STORIES
— FROM —
VERMONT'S
MARBLE VALLEY

STORIES
— FROM —
VERMONT'S
MARBLE VALLEY

MIKE AUSTIN

THE
History
PRESS

Published by The History Press
Charleston, SC 29403
www.historypress.net

Cover images courtesy of the Rutland Historical Society.

First published 2010

Manufactured in the United States

ISBN 978.1.59629.925.2

Austin, Mike, Ph. D.
Stories from Vermont's Marble Valley / Mike Austin.
p. cm.
Includes bibliographical references.
ISBN 978-1-59629-925-2
1. Marble industry and trade--Vermont--Rutland County--History--Anecdotes. 2.
Quarries and quarrying--Vermont--Rutland County--History--Anecdotes. 3. Mills and
mill-work--Vermont--Rutland County--History--Anecdotes. 4. Working class--Vermont--
Rutland County--History--Anecdotes. 5. Rutland County (Vt.)--History, Local--Anecdotes.
6. Rutland County (Vt.)--Economic conditions--Anecdotes. I. Title.
HD9621.7.U63R883 2010
974.3'7--dc22
2010006754

CONTENTS

PREFACE

Some may think of writing a book as a solitary experience in which an author faces all by himself or herself a fearful, daunting white page. The concept of a manuscript may start with the author in the form of a question, as it did in the case of this book: "How did the Marble Valley of Vermont come to be the way it is?" Historians are intellectual detectives, searching out present-day clues to see how things have come about. Unlike modern detectives, who are limited to interviewing contemporaries, historians "interview" people and documents from previous times and have a team of collaborators helping them tell the story.

So, I want to thank Dr. J. William Harris of the University of New Hampshire, who helped to guide me in my early research. Mr. James Davidson of the Rutland Historical Society in Vermont helped both in the early and later stages. Ms. Mary Fergosi, history teacher extraordinaire and an executive board member of the Rutland Historical Society, and Nancy Kennedy, not just a librarian but the very epitome of a librarian and also an executive board member of the Proctor Historical Society—both of Proctor, Vermont—helped to inform me of further details of the marble story.

When I presented material in public forums, helpful people shared stories of their family's involvement. The Dimensions of Marble Executive Committee—Lee Khan, president; Beth Meachem; Linda Doty, treasurer; Lisa Johnson; Marcia Chioffi; and especially Cathy Miglorie, assistant director of the Vermont Marble Museum—encouraged the publication of this work. In addition, the advisory board of Dimensions of Marble was very helpful: Robert Pye of the Vermont Marble Museum; Stephen A. Carbine; Lindsey Johnson; Carol Driscoll of the International Carving Studio of West Rutland, Vermont; Caro Thompson, a documentary filmmaker; and the Advisory International Board chair, Virginia Russell.

In the actual writing, beyond Dr. Harris there were many others who helped and should be acknowledged: first of all, Elizabeth Cusulas, Mary Giordano and Lani Duke were the principal word angels who suggested clarification of ideas; Anne Tait of Roger Williams University offered discussions and encouragement about memorial artwork in the use of marble; and Anne Kennedy Ilacqua, former librarian at Brown University, assisted as well. In helping to get the information to the publisher, Scott Hanselman, Bobby Burge, Sarah Backus, Karen Sanborn and Lauren Olewnk of Castleton State College were very helpful, and I am indebted to them and to Professor Andy Alexander, also of Castleton State College, for encouragement. Steve Eddy, the former owner of Book King, a local bookstore, encouraged a wider audience for this material.

At The History Press, I am indebted to Brianna Cullen, who went out of her way so many times to be supportive, and to Ryan Finn, whose incisive writing insights also immeasurably improved this book.

And finally, a public acknowledgement to the intriguing historical place in which I live. The Marble Valley of Vermont, in name and public buildings both exterior and interior, is like a large museum that proudly displays its cultural heritage and the importance of marble to the region. In particular, the Vermont Marble Museum in Proctor and the International Carving Studio in West Rutland continue to celebrate the story of marble's history and contemporary influence. It is a story that helps visitors and residents appreciate the region and how it came to be. This is a fascinating tale of the people who helped settle a region and carve out a new identity and heritage there, framed by a paramount sense of place.

This book is dedicated to Kerry Austin-Smith and Molly Anne Austin, two very wonderful daughters who have spent their formative years growing up in the Marble Valley of Vermont.

CHAPTER 1

SETTLING A VALLEY

Understanding the Sense of Place

Like an explorer or early settler—or a more adventurous modern-day tourist or resident—you can travel from the comfort of your armchair into a valley rich in history and shaped by trade, war and settlement. Rival confederations of indigenous peoples fought for dominance. Then European powers arrived and continued the rivalries that lasted three hundred years.[1]

With the arrival of the Europeans, religion, immigrant groups and geography played important roles in helping to forge Vermont's identity. The Marble Valley runs from Middlebury in the north to Dorset in the south. It is home to the largest marble company in the world, the Vermont Marble Company, headquartered in Proctor, Vermont, which is also the site of the Vermont Marble Museum, the largest museum in the world devoted to that subject. Proctor is not the only Vermont community in which marble continues to play a major role, though. West Rutland contains the internationally recognized Carving Studio & Sculpture Center; both studio and gallery are open to the public. Understanding the historical context will help you to appreciate the region and seek out areas you might want to know better.

Even before the European settlement, northern New England—especially the western section in what is now Vermont—had been an uncertain territory, precarious for permanent settlement and a land bordered by rival Native confederations. These tribes aligned themselves with the French, English and Dutch, playing off the Europeans for their own interests.

With the end of the French and Indian War in the fall of 1759, the French menace to New England ceased. The English and the colonials had

Site of the Vermont Marble Company mill. Now it is the site of the Vermont Marble Museum, which provides a history of the company, as well as current and historic uses of marble. The museum houses many marble gifts and souvenirs for tourists. *Mike Austin Collection.*

captured the French capital, Quebec, the seat of French economic, military and political power in North America. In the British colonies, great bonfires were lit in celebration of the victory. Lasting peace, it seemed, was at hand. The last frontier of New England, from the British perspective, could now finally be opened up free of the menace of the Catholic French.

Over the next two decades, the longstanding and often bitter dispute over whether this region belonged to New Hampshire or New York gradually subsided. Traveling Crown Point Road, an east–west connection crossing New Hampshire and Vermont and eventually linking with New York, had familiarized colonial soldiers with the land of what is now Rutland, Vermont. By 1759, the land was opening up for real estate speculators.

Running in a southeast–northwest direction, Crown Point Road passed through a broad valley oriented north–south between the Green Mountains on the east and the Taconic Mountains on the west—a valley being continually reshaped by the vigorous Otter Creek and its tributaries.[2] The Crown Point Association has helped to erect historical signs throughout the region, so if you enjoy hiking, you can explore parts of this historic trail. The area's many northerly trending rivers and floodplains had served as natural transportation routes for pre-settlement Native Americans; the succeeding generations of colonists found themselves using many of the same natural passages, not yet realizing that vast deposits of marble lay underneath.[3]

Benning Wentworth, colonial governor of New Hampshire from 1741 to 1766, issued the writ that defined Rutland Town in 1761. *Courtesy of Rutland Historical Society.*

Four more years would drag on before a final peace treaty was signed in Paris in 1763, officially ending the French and Indian War. The time lag did not deter avid colonial speculators from making claims to the land. Benning Wentworth, the royal governor of New Hampshire, viewed the territory, with a mixture of political bravado and financial gain, as an extension of New Hampshire and set about issuing grants throughout the region. The Rutland Charter set aside twenty-six thousand acres, about six square miles.[4]

On Monday, September 7, 1761, George III's charter for Rutland Town set the conditions for settlement "[w]ith the advice of our trusty and well-beloved Benning Wentworth, our governor and commander-in-chief of our said Province of New Hampshire."[5] In the charter, each grant was to set aside an area for the Anglican Church; when you travel throughout Vermont, notice that prominent communities contain a Church Street, often the original site of the Anglican church in the town.

Later, rival European settlements of the Dutch, the English and the French increased the complexity of the constant conflict. Until these macro conflicts were resolved, it was a dangerous place for permanent settlement, but even afterward the trouble would not be over. By military conquest, the English had won the rights to the region, but that only set off another round of conflicts among the colonies of New York, Massachusetts and New Hampshire—each of which claimed part or all of the land. The colony of Massachusetts Bay had expansionist tendencies and at one time encompassed the area of Maine and New Hampshire, as well as Massachusetts. In 1713, Massachusetts was found guilty of granting lands of 110,000 acres that belonged to the colony of Connecticut. An arrangement was worked out between the colonies, and the region known as the Equivalent Lands was sold in Hartford, Connecticut, at the courthouse on April 24 and 25, 1715, with the proceeds given to the then twelve-year-old college of Yale. So the colony of Vermont helped to establish Yale College.

William Brattle and William Dummer were both major Massachusetts speculators in the land deal, and the territory remained under Massachusetts jurisdiction. Eventually, the territory became separated from Massachusetts, but Brattle's and Dummer's names remained in the grants as Brattleboro and Dummerston.[6]

Because of the potential for dangerous conflict and the uncertain validity of the land claims, settlement in the region lagged behind that of the other New England colonies. Speculators, mostly from New York and New Hampshire, began to shape the political landscape. The shapers at first were the elites, the large speculators and granters of land, such as Governor Lord Dunmore (John Murray), Willliam Tryon and Cadwallader Colden of New York and Benning Wentworth of New Hampshire.

Gradually, the settlers began to make an impression on the land. From various sections of New England (especially Connecticut) and beyond (especially New York), speculators and settlers came to the land to claim and develop it.[7] The New York patents were especially nettlesome to the New Englanders.[8] The settlers came west from New Hampshire on Crown Point

Road; north up the Connecticut River, then westward and then north from western Connecticut along the Deerfield River into the Green Mountains and into southwestern Vermont; or north up the Housatonic River to the Berkshires, entering Vermont in its far southwest.

The land offered opportunity to reward the most bold and enterprising.[9] James Mead was the first settler in Rutland. He had migrated from Nine Partners, New York, to Manchester, Vermont, in 1764. In 1769, he built a cabin at Center Rutland near the Otter Creek's "little falls," where he would soon build a gristmill. In March 1770, he brought his wife, ten children and a son-in-law to the house, encircled by ice and floodwater from Otter Creek at the time. An Indian allowed Mead's family to stay the night in a wigwam.

John William Sutherland, another early settler, had enlisted in the Seventy-seventh Regiment of foot soldiers during the French and Indian War and had become acquainted with the Rutland region when he was stationed at Crown Point. He grasped the strategic importance of the Otter Creek and, in particular, the Great Falls six miles north of the Mead property. In the spring of 1775, he purchased more than three hundred acres surrounding the Great Falls and constructed a sawmill and gristmill at the falls, staying there for nearly twenty years until 1793. He sold most of the property on Otter Creek to his son, Peter; that area of the Rutland grant subsequently was referred to as Sutherland Falls. Later, this area would be renamed Proctor because of the political and economic influence of Proctor and the marble industry.

Perceived by his neighbors as untrustworthy, John Sutherland had a reputation as an opportunist. A neighbor spoke of him:

> *He was on ordinary terms with his neighbors and carried on his gristmill; but it cannot be denied that tradition has given him the name of being selfish and grasping; one story being that at the time of the battle of Hubbardton, when so many of the settlers left their homes and sought protection at Bennington, they were forced to leave their swine roaming at large. They branded the animals and turned them into the woods. On their return they found some of their pigs in Mr. Sutherland's pen.*[10]

Sutherland may have sided with the Tories during the early part of the Revolutionary War, but by 1778–79, he and his sons were serving in the American militia. Although Ethan Allen regarded him with suspicion,

Sutherland remained protected because of his influence, strategic property in the region and, above all, his vital mill.[11]

Benjamin Whipple and Timothy Boardman and their families were among the first developers of another section of Rutland, later known as West Rutland. There is a major organic farm located on Boardman Hill[12] in West Rutland today; during the summer season, it has wonderful fresh vegetables and produce and is worth a stop.

Such settlers came into the valley about the time of the Revolutionary War, trekking north from Massachusetts and Connecticut. In 1761, Whipple and his wife Hepzibah migrated from Massachusetts to Bennington, Vermont, just over the Massachusetts border, following the traditional path north on Route 7, which stretched from Connecticut to Montreal. Many Connecticut migrants traveled this corridor from Connecticut through western Massachusetts and north up the Connecticut River Valley and into Vermont, paralleling the Green Mountains to the west. By 1776, the Whipples had settled in Rutland. A section of West Rutland bears the name Whipple Hollow.[13]

Born in Middletown, Connecticut, Timothy Boardman had experiences similar to those of Benjamin Whipple. Boardman was a soldier in the Continental army, a captain with Washington at Dorchester Heights and an assistant quartermaster at the surrender of Burgoyne in October 1777. In 1782, he arrived in Rutland, where he bought one hundred acres of land from the estate of Reverend Benajah Roots, building himself a small frame house. In the fall, he returned to Connecticut to bring his new wife to their house on what is now referred to as Boardman Hill in West Rutland. Like the other settlers of the valley near Otter Creek, he was a Congregationalist, and he served as a deacon of the Congregational church in the west parish in West Rutland (1782–1839).

Besides the spirit of opportunity, most of the earliest settlers in the valley, like Boardman, brought with them Congregationalism. On October 20, 1773, a Congregational church was organized near the falls at Center Rutland, followed a short time later by a meetinghouse on Pleasant Street's "Meeting House Hill" in West Rutland.[14] The area was Protestant, with pockets of deistic sympathizers in Burlington and Fair Haven. The Vermont Constitution of 1777 reinforced a Protestant ideology, barring from office those who did not "profess the Protestant religion."[15] Enforced for nearly a decade, the provision was dropped in 1786.

To some believers, deistic thinkers posed a threat to the dominance of the Congregational authority. Reverend Nathan Perkins, aware of the deistic thinkers in the valley, set out in 1789 on a journey to bring salvation to the "unchurched" freethinkers of Vermont. Lodgings were few and far between. Staying at Mr. Flint's in Brandon, he noted that it was the "meanest of all lodging,—dirty,—fleas without number." Because of the poor roads, oftentimes he was lost in woods and forests, where he shivered at "ye horrible howling of ye wolves. Brook-water is my chief drink. The maple cyder is horrible stuff—no malt in ye Country.—Their beer poor bran beer."[16] But if you are exploring today, be sure to have some maple cider or at least apple cider, especially in the fall.

In the 1780s, more religious diversity began to emerge. Episcopalians arrived in Vermont in the 1780s. In March 1784, Reverend Chittenden, brother of the governor, delivered a sermon on the Episcopal Society at the statehouse in Rutland. In that year, on September 30, a Protestant Episcopal church was formed.[17] Twenty-four state Episcopalian delegates met in 1793 in Pawlet, in the southwestern part of Rutland County, to seek a bishop for the state.

In the 1790s and 1800s, Celtic names such as Kelley, Gleason, Butler and Barrett appear in local records. In the late 1700s, these men were small farmers from Protestant (and Presbyterian) Ulster who settled on farms in Shrewsbury, Tinmouth, Wallingford and in other parts of the Rutland valley. Some found employment at the ironworks in Pittsford. This minor immigration continued into the 1840s. Overall, however, in both Rutland and in the state as a whole, 95 percent of the settlers stemmed from English stock.[18] Traveling through Vermont in 1798, Timothy Dwight, the president of Yale, found the future Marble Valley particularly inhospitable. Describing the valley around Middlebury, he wrote of the soil:

> In wet seasons every rain converts it into mud. Whenever the weather is dry, it is pulverized wherever mankind live and move; and the dust, being very fine and light, rises with every wind, fills the air with clouds, covers the houses, and soils the clothes with a dingy, dirty appearance. When the surface of well-made roads has become hard, a slight rain makes them so slippery as to be impassable with safety, unless with horses corked in the same manner as when they are to travel on ice.[19]

Faced with these conditions, Vermonters sought to improve them. In the first decade of the nineteenth century, a road-building fever swept Rutland County. In 1800, a road between Middlebury and Woodstock was chartered; the Hubbardton Turnpike, chartered in 1802, authorized a road from Hubbardton to Castleton; and the Poultney Turnpike was chartered in 1805, extending from Castleton to the New York line in Poultney. The Fair Haven Turnpike, running from Fair Haven to the town of Bridport, was also chartered in 1805. Transportation improvements helped to spur population growth; between 1800 and 1810, Rutland Town grew from 2,125 to 23,813.[20]

With settlement, more Protestant denominations established themselves. Methodism, because it had grown so rapidly and seemed so emotional, caused bitter resentment among the more disciplined Calvinists. By 1799, Joseph Mitchel and Joseph Sawyer were on the Methodist Vergennes circuit, traveling as many as four hundred miles and rotating throughout the region on a four-week cycle. By 1801, the Methodist influence had grown enough that the denomination established a Brandon Circuit, an area just north of Rutland and well within the valley. About 1815, Jacob Beaman was a circuit rider. "He was a ready speaker, full of zeal and energy—a lover of Methodism, and an ardent hater of Calvinism. To the last days of his preaching, in his old age, he would strike hard blows against Calvin in every sermon."[21]

Local historian Abby Maria Hemenway noted the bitter response of the Congregationalists:

> *It is a little strange that Methodism should encounter stronger hostility than any other system—Deism, Mormonism, free love—indeed any other thing which has arisen, has never suffered the opposition, and even persecution that Methodists have endured in nearly all places. At West Rutland a father gave his son a most brutal flogging for uniting with them! And that father lives there even now.*[22]

The Methodists were not the only new evangelical denomination. On Friday, August 17, 1804, thirty-five residents of Rutland met at the home of Amos Weller to form the First Baptist Society of Rutland. A Baptist church was organized in Center Rutland on Friday, January 11, 1805. Because of migration and deaths, the membership, however, declined.[23]

Even as a new century began, most population growth continued to take place in the southern part of the state rather than in the middle or the northern regions. Guilford in 1800 was the largest town, followed by Bennington, but Windsor, Woodstock and Rutland, all in the center of the state along an east–west axis, had begun to grow. By 1800, Rutland Town had achieved fifth position with a population of 2,125. Travel, however, was still difficult throughout the state.

Lacking adequate roads to transport their products, farmers had little incentive to expand far beyond what would feed their families and the families of nearby service or small-scale merchandise providers. This first stage was self-sufficiency. Later, a small surplus could be sold to larger markets. A Vermont farmer, with his and his neighbor's farm goods, would travel to the large market in Boston and sell the goods there and at the same time have the opportunity to purchase store goods. T. Hands, writing from southern New Hampshire, observed:

> *In the winter from 50 to 100 sleighs pass from Vermont in the upper part of this state to Boston with dead hogs, pork, butter, cheese, etc., and load back with store goods. They have generally 2 horses and travel 40 miles a day with a ton weight.*[21]

Napoleon's invasion of Spain, half a world away, would prompt the next step in the development of the valley from self-sufficiency and some marketing to specialized production. To pay off debts, wealthy Spanish landowners were forced to sell off some of their prized Merino sheep. William Jarvis, the American consul at Lisbon, acquired permission to export two hundred Merino rams of the Escurial Royal flock in 1809; he returned to Boston in 1810. The following year, he moved to Weathersfield Bow, about twenty miles north of Bellows Falls, Vermont, along the Connecticut River. By 1820, descendants of the royal Merinos had helped Vermont's sheep industry become the most profitable industry in the state. The dramatic growth of the sheep industry also aided in developing ancillary industries. Rutland County in 1837 led all other counties with the most sheep, 180,984; next was Windsor with 171,581, and just north of Rutland County was Addison with 159,411. The remaining eleven counties had fewer than 100,000.[25]

The sheep industry, for a time, was a bulwark against the general agricultural decline that followed the financial panic of 1837.[26]

In the late 1840s, the sheep industry fell into its own sharp decline. Vermont, at one point second in the nation in sheep production, was now at a price disadvantage with wool from the West. From the 1840s onward, there was a steady decline in profitability. To prosper, Rutland needed to shift its economic base and needed a better transportation infrastructure to do so. Throughout the region, you may see some remaining mills and sheep farms, some dating back to this time period.

Hoping to stimulate further development, Vermonters became caught up in the national craze of canal building. The Champlain Canal in New York was constructed in 1823 and the Erie Canal, two years later. Local entrepreneurs thought that Otter Creek might serve as a base for a canal to New York, some twenty miles distant. In 1825, the Vermont legislature chartered the Otter Creek and Castleton River Canal Company. Moses Strong and Francis Slason of Rutland were two of the twenty-one incorporators, along with John Conant of Brandon. Strong was the group's chair. The chief obstacle to a canal was the Great Falls at Sutherland, which would necessitate expensive locks if it were to be navigated. As it turned out, this was the first of many transportation schemes that went nowhere. Engineers considered the cost, but nothing concrete emerged.[27]

On January 15, 1830, a meeting in Montpelier studied the possibility of a railway from Boston to Lake Champlain. Rutland meetings as early as 1831 also discussed railroad building. The Rutland-Whitehall Railroad, planned to link to the Champlain canal system, was chartered on November 9, 1831, but failed to produce any physical construction. At Matthew Birchard's Inn at Brandon on September 4, 1835, a group of citizens from Middlebury, Salisbury, Brandon, Pittsford and Rutland met to discuss railroads. The specific agenda was to discuss "the most practical route for a railroad from Middlebury to Market." One of the attendees, John A. Conant of Brandon, very much aware of the earlier canal craze, was known as a hard-dealing businessman who favored the railroad. He eventually proved to be instrumental in lobbying the legislature for a northern route. The group, encouraged by the very practical Conant, resolved to propose that an "application be made to the Legislature, October 2, 1835 for a grant of a Railroad from Middlebury, in the County of Addison, through the Valley of Otter Creek, to intersect the [still unbuilt] Rutland and Whitehall Railroad at Rutland in the County of Rutland."[28]

By 1835, the legislature had issued several charters for railroads throughout the state. Because no construction had taken place under the old charter, the Rutland-Whitehall Railroad required re-chartering. Issued in November 1836, the new charter for the Rutland-Whitehall Railroad authorized a capital of $250,000 for construction. However, when the financial panic of 1837 hit, it most directly affected the railroad, delaying construction even though the stock had been sold and the route surveyed.[29] In the aftermath of the 1837 panic, and lacking railroad development, Vermont's economy had stagnated. In the 1830s and 1840s, many traditional Protestant Yankees had left Vermont. The Midwest was more attractive, drawing the younger generation to its fertile and level plains.[30] Migration from Vermont reached its zenith from the 1830s to the 1870s. A letter writer to the *Rutland Herald* recounted his experience moving west:

> *In 1836 I was* en route *over the half way station of Freedom. During that, and the preceding year—"Going to Michigan" was plainly daguerreotyped nine-tenths of the travelers moving through and from Vermont. You could see the place of destination in the countenance as plan as the nose on the fact—but, as Sam Slick used to say—"it stuck out all around." The Michigan Emigration fever proved to be the prevailing epidemic in '36 throughout the New England States—in Vermont particularly, taking off scores of families—and individuals, young and old, (I among the number), hundreds of whom date back to the event as the commencement of a series of Life Scenes upon which some cast retrospective glances with thankfulness, while these less fortunate in the result of emigration look back upon the move as the most disastrous event of their history. Health and prosperity cheered the one, while sickness and misfortune and want were the unwelcome attendants of the other.*[31]

An economy that would facilitate trade needed to be developed. By the end of 1842, plans were underway to survey a railroad route that would connect Boston to Lake Champlain. George T. Hodges chaired, and Jonathan C. Dexter was secretary for a meeting held at the Rutland Courthouse on January 11, 1843. As with canal building, which demanded locks for difficult sections, and as at Sutherland Falls, where the geography ultimately led to the demise of a Rutland canal, the issue for the railroads was geography: whether the available engines could negotiate the mountains. Conventional wisdom dictated that, although track laying was feasible in relatively level areas, it was out of the question in Vermont's mountainous terrain.

On January 3, 1843, the *Rutland Herald* argued for the necessity of the railroad:

> *We are an inland State, rich in mineral manufacturing and agricultural resources—out of debt and running over with abundance—yet poor, because*

we cannot profitably carry the surplus to market, for cash. In addition to this, all heavy articles of import cost us a large percentage above the retail price on the seaboard in consequence of the slow, tedious and expensive method of transportation. We suffer a complication of disadvantages which makes us poor and will keep us poor until we overcome them by creating ample facilities for cheap intercourse with [the] market and place ourselves on a footing of equality with our competitors.[32]

By August 1843, the *Herald* was able to report with excitement:

The corps of engineers now surveying a route for the railroad from Rutland to the Connecticut River takes this method of expressing their thanks to the inhabitants bordering on the route for the generous hospitality evidenced by them, also for the liberal aid in personally assisting them in the work.[33]

In October of that year, Senator Ebenezer Briggs of Brandon introduced "An Act to Incorporate the Champlain and Connecticut River Rail Road Company." Still, progress was slow. Not until the spring of 1845 was the westernmost of the proposed routes selected, on the grounds that it would be twenty-five minutes shorter. On May 6, 1845, with Timothy Follett of Burlington as chair and Ambrose L. Brown as clerk, the Champlain and Connecticut River Rail Road stockholders selected nine directors, and the board voted to sell stock on June 10. The excitement of the project was contagious. Within two days, two thousand shares had been sold at the George T. Hodges store in Rutland. In January 1846, more than two thousand men attended a meeting at the Rutland Courthouse; it was so crowded that the meeting was adjourned to a nearby church. William B. Gilbert, the chief engineer, and George W. Strong, an advocate of a railroad between Rutland and Bennington, spoke. That year, construction finally got underway.[34]

For an illustration of Don Quixote tilting at an engine of the line, the *Rutland Herald* for December 3, 1846, commented:

Our purpose in presenting this engraving to our readers is simply to illustrate folly to say nothing of the danger of any further opposition to the Rutland Railroad. And if there are any among us who from sectional or personal feeling, still feel a disposition to manifest an opposition to the advancement of this great enterprise…if there are any who yet lack faith in the belief

*that the czars are coming…to all such we would dare to look at the above,
and take heed! The snort of the dreaded monster is already heard…the bell
is ringing and if you won't do anything else…in all conscience, for your
own safety, clear the track.*[35]

With this enthusiasm, even in mountainous Vermont, 250 miles of railroad
track were laid between 1846 and 1849. On January 28, 1846, construction
for what would be the Central Vermont Railroad began at Northfield; the
line would link White River Junction, the end of the line from Concord, New
Hampshire, with Burlington, 104 miles northwest. The Central Vermont
Railroad was in competition with the Rutland Railroad; both railroads saw
Burlington as a vital link.

In August 1846, William Gilbert, the Rutland line's chief engineer,
reported that he had almost completed the survey of the sixty-five miles
between Rutland and Burlington and estimated the cost for grading, masonry
and bridging to be $400,000. In order to make the company more appealing
and to attract more capital, the board changed the name in November
1847, reflecting on the two population centers of the state, and the company
became known as the Rutland and Burlington Railroad. Construction of
the Rutland Railroad (as it apparently was most popularly known) began on
January 28, 1847, one year behind the Central Vermont, with a link between
Bellows Falls and Burlington. On May 1, 1847, construction began on the
section between Burlington and Brandon.[36]

By 1849, the Rutland and Burlington Railroad system had been
completed. During the 1850s, when practically every community in the
East and Midwest competed to secure a railroad, three railroad lines
connected Rutland to Troy and Albany, New York, and from there to other
railroads connecting to Canada and Boston. The coming of the railroad
in Vermont after 1850 opened up opportunities for the mining, quarrying
and manufacturing industries. By 1852, four railroad lines entered Rutland,
two of which passed through West Rutland: the Rutland and Washington
Railroad and the Rensselaer and Saratoga. The Rutland and Washington
Railroad went from Rutland, Castleton, Poultney, Rupert and Salem to
Troy, New York, and the Rensselaer and Saratoga went from Whitehall and
Saratoga to Troy.[37] For contemporary explorers, the old railroad station at
Castleton, the Depot, contains a wonderful bakery, highly recommended for
breakfast and lunch.

The railroad, and the developing marble industry that it made possible, would transform the valley in profound ways. Prior to 1852, before the railroad came to the Rutland area, marble was hauled by horses or oxen to the lake and the canal in Whitehall, New York, for shipment to other markets. Because of the cost of such transportation and the limitations of the horses or oxen, the amount of marble shipped out of the area was small. The building of the railroads helped to solve many of the transportation problems for the marble industry. In 1839, for example, marble production in West Rutland quarries was valued at barely $10,000, but a little more than a decade later, by 1850, the value had risen to $297,000.[38] The marble industry—with more workers, more demand and better transportation—had entered a boom cycle.

As some were exiting the state for better farmlands, others, especially immigrants, arrived to build the railroad. In February 1847, Irish immigrants began to work on the railroad at Rockingham and, in May, at Burlington. In that decade, concentrated numbers of Irish began to settle in the Rutland area. Although a few Irish had arrived during the 1830s, the immigration wave of the 1840s was vastly larger.

These later Irish, often from the western parts of Ireland, had been displaced and driven out of Ireland by a series of events. In the mid-1830s, English landlords had raised the rent to a price tenants could not pay; many "struck" their landlord, refusing to pay rent at all. Second, the 1846–50 potato blight decimated the potato crop, worsening the situation. Families were not only unable to pay rent, but they were also unable to afford food. They suffered under appalling conditions. To this generation of Irish, even rudimentary company housing must have seemed heavenly. Contemporary William Bennett wrote of the human misery he saw in Ireland in 1847:

> Many of the cabins were holes in the bog, covered with a layer of turves, and not distinguishable as human habitations from the surrounding moor, until close down upon them. The bare sod was about the best material of which any of them were constructed. Doorways, not doors, were usually provided at both sides of the bettermost—back and front—to take advantage of the way of the wind. Windows and chimneys, I think, had no existence.
>
> A second apartment or division of any kind within was exceedingly rare. Furniture, properly so called, I believe may be stated at nil. I would not speak with certainty, and wish not to with exaggeration,—we were too

much overcome to note specifically; but as far as memory serves, we saw neither bed, chair, nor table, at all...

The scenes of human misery and degradation we witnessed still haunt my imagination, with the vividness and power of some horrid and tyrannous delusion, rather than the features of a sober reality. We entered a cabin.

Stretched in one dark corner, scarcely visible, from the smoke and rags that covered them, were three children huddled together, lying there because they were too weak to rise, pale and ghastly, their little limbs—on removing a portion of the filthy covering—perfectly emaciated, eyes sunk, voice gone, and evidently in the last stage of actual starvation. Crouched over the turf embers was another form, wild and all but naked, scarcely human in appearance. It stirred not, nor noticed us.

On some straw, soddened upon the ground, moaning piteously, was a shrivelled old woman, imploring us to give her something,—baring her limbs partly, to show how the skin hung loose from the bones, as soon as she attracted our attention. Above her, on something like a ledge, was a young woman, with sunken cheeks,—a mother I have no doubt,—who scarcely raised her eyes in answer to our enquiries, but pressed her hand upon her forehead, with a look of unutterable anguish and despair.

Many cases were widows, whose husbands had recently been taken off by the fever, and thus their only pittance, obtained from the public works entirely cut off. In many the husbands or sons were prostrate, under that horrid disease,—the results of long-continued famine and low living,—in which first the limbs, and then the body, swell most frightfully, and finally burst...It was my full impression that one-fourth of those we saw were in a dying state, beyond the reach of any relief that could now be afforded; and many more would follow.[39]

Leaving their dead behind, Irish families came to Vermont and other parts of New England looking for a new life. Many of those from County Roscommon, in western Ireland, crossed the Atlantic on one of four "coffin ships"; a significant number failed to complete the crossing, dying at sea. Those who agreed to sign over ancestral titles to their Irish properties frequently had their fare paid by the British government, a form of "state-aided immigration." Once in New England, some Irish came to Vermont as part of railroad track–laying crews, settling into company housing at the marble quarries. As many as forty-seven families from Roscommon County, for instance, worked in the Dorset and Rutland town marble quarries at the time of the 1860 federal census.[40]

The French Canadian Catholics were the other major immigrant group that arrived in the valley in the first half of the nineteenth century. Their immigration was similar to that of the Irish. Crop failures, overpopulation and political persecution to the north initially brought some three hundred French Canadian families into Vermont in 1808. In 1837 and 1838, the Papineau rebellions drove more French into Vermont, at least on a temporary basis.[11] The French Canadians gradually worked their way south, drawn by jobs in the more industrialized communities. By 1840, Catholic Masses were being said in private homes in Burlington, St. Albans, Rutland, Middlebury, Bennington, Swanton, Castleton and Randolph.[12] Three of those eight towns—Rutland, Middlebury and Castleton—were part of the Marble Valley or very closely associated with it. Lacking sufficient numbers of Catholic worshipers in any one community, priests infrequently traveled to Vermont towns to celebrate Mass.[13]

Although Vermont did not have a large immigrant population, the presence of any immigrant group, especially one that was not Protestant, posed a threat to some. The Irish were the first of the foreign-born, non-English groups to come to the Marble Valley in large numbers, settling in the northwest part of Rutland (later given the name of Proctor) and in other sections of Rutland. So many settled in such concentrated numbers in the section of Rutland known as West Rutland that it became known as "Little Ireland."[14]

Tragically, many of these same families, evicted in Ireland and forced to sign over any rights to their land by their British landlord, Lord Heartland, found themselves evicted again from their houses in their new homeland in 1867. In the second general marble strike, the workers struck for better working conditions, and once more they were evicted in such numbers that they referred to it as "the great turn-out."

With the growth of marble and with it the influx of population, the twenty-year decline of Rutland, between 1830 and 1850, began to change dramatically in the decade of the 1850s.[15] In 1800, the population of Rutland had been 2,124. By 1850, it reached 3,715, half the size of Burlington.[16] With the advent of the railroad and the burgeoning marble industry, however, Rutland was poised for dramatic social, political and economic growth, which would give the valley a new identity: the Marble Valley.

CHAPTER 2

TRANSFORMING A VALLEY
INTO THE MARBLE VALLEY

When constructing a railroad in 1849 from Rutland to Burlington in Charlotte, Vermont, workers came across a perplexing mystery. About ten feet below the surface, they unearthed the remains of a strange animal. The skeleton turned out to be a marine animal, a "beluga" or "white" whale, an animal that normally inhabits arctic and subarctic marine waters in the northern hemisphere. But how could a whale be in landlocked Vermont? The dramatic story of the whale in present-day Vermont becomes even more remarkable. Evidence shows that a warm, shallow sea, the Iapetus Ocean, covered a large portion of what today would be eastern North America, from New England and eastern Canada to the Midwest as far as Michigan and north into midwestern Canada.[17] The dramatic story of the Marble Valley begins with the Iapetus Ocean, which is 500 million years older than the Atlantic Ocean.

About 350 million years ago, the Iapetus Ocean closed up—the sedimentary rock of the shoreline and the continental shelf folded under pressure and created faults, resulting in formation of the Appalachian Mountains and, in our region, the Green Mountains (part of the Appalachian chain, which extends along most of the East Coast of the United States). The heat and pressure caused by the formation of these mountains provided the conditions necessary for calcium carbonate to metamorphose into marble.

About 12,500 years ago, melting glaciers created a freshwater basin now referred to as Lake Vermont. About 10,000 years ago, receding glaciers opened a path allowing salt water from the St. Lawrence into the basin, creating the Champlain Sea as an arm of the Atlantic Ocean. More portions of modern-day Vermont were soon under a large body of water, resulting in sea animals' skeletons contributing to the calcium carbonate as they drifted to the bottom. As the glaciers retreated farther, the connection to the St. Lawrence closed again, and the sea gradually reverted to a smaller body of fresh water we now know as Lake Champlain.

All of these pressurized forces contributed to the formation of the region's marble. The marble in Vermont lies in a lowland, called the Marble Valley, located between two waterways. To the west is the Castleton River, flowing parallel to the Otter Creek from Florence to West Rutland. Meandering westward at West Rutland, the river flows out of the Marble Valley and into the town of Castleton and beyond to the rich slate belt area of Vermont and New York. The Slate Valley Museum in Granville, New York, offers visitors a look at the history of the slate industry in this region. East of the valley, the Otter Creek runs from Dorset, at the northern end of Bennington County, to Middlebury, at the southern end of Addison County, emptying into Lake Champlain west of Vergennes. As it passes through the heart of the Marble Valley, the Otter Creek flows through one of the richest deposits of marble in the world. These deposits lie in a belt slightly skewed in a northwest–southeast direction. The richest section of the mineral deposits lies in the area between the Taconic and

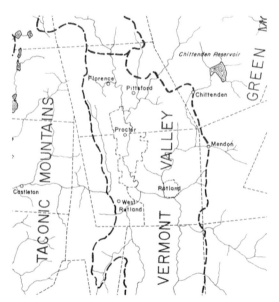

The Marble Valley is nestled between the Taconic Mountains to the west and the Green Mountains to the east. The Vermont Valley would become the heart of the Marble Valley. *Courtesy of Vermont Water Resources Department.*

the Green Mountains, in the heart of the Marble Valley—from Brandon in the north through Florence and Proctor to end in the south at West Rutland.

The Marble Valley itself extends from Middlebury in the north to Dorset in the south.[18] Most early marble quarry sites in the area developed at outcroppings where the marble was on or just below the surface. Development of the marble industry was gradual and secondary to other enterprises. At first, marble's primary use was as monument stone.

In Dorset, at the southern end of the Marble Valley, some marble gravestones bear memorial inscriptions from as early as 1785. Isaac Underhill, who opened a quarry site in Vermont in 1785, found other uses for his marble, such as fire jambs, chimney blocks and hearths and lintels for the massive fireplaces of the day.[19] Dorset is the site of the largest underground marble quarry in the world.

Even before 1800, thirty-two-year-old Rutland lawyer Nathaniel Chipman had proposed a broader, more commercial vision for marble production. In

Rows of modern-day grave markers are lined up, ready for their individual inscriptions. *Courtesy of Vermont Marble Museum.*

a letter to General Philip Schuyler of New York, dated January 25, 1792, Chipman speculated on the potential: "There are also in this part of the country numerous quarries of marble some of them of superior quality. Machines may easily be erected for sawing it into slabs by water, and in that state it might become an important article of commerce."[50]

By 1794, quarrying in Rutland County had begun operation on a limited basis, but Rutland lagged behind Dorset, in Bennington County, by almost a decade. That year, Alexander Ralstone and Jonathan Wells deeded the first Rutland County quarry to Ebenezer Blanchard. It was located in West Rutland, west of today's Clarendon Avenue and south of Route 4, Main Street.[51]

About the turn of the nineteenth century, more small-scale marble activity began. In 1795, Lorenzo Sheldon opened a second quarry in Rutland County, a little farther north, along the Otter Creek in Pittsford. Then a series of small entrepreneurs began to enter the market. In 1799, Eli Hudson opened a second quarry in Pittsford, and in 1806 Charles Lamb opened the third quarry in the Pittsford area.[52] Ezra Meach leased the mineral rights from Timothy Brockway and opened the True Blue Quarry in 1807 in Whipple Hollow of West Rutland, while Brockway continued to use the land for himself as a farm. In May 1807, Brockway entered into another alliance and reversed the situation. He separated quarrying rights from land ownership, deeding the property to Alexander Donahue but reserving the right to extract marble until 1809.[53]

Small-scale marble operations continued to spread. In 1808, Elijah Sykes opened a quarry known as Wilson, McDonald and Freedly's Quarry. John Chapman and Abraham Underhill purchased it from Sykes in 1810. Several of the marble entrepreneurs noted the excellent quality of stone that Luther Perkins had produced from a quarry on the road between the meetinghouse and Pittsford, now known as Pleasant Street. The quarry was west of the road, east of the swamp and two and a half miles from Pleasant Street and old Route 4 in West Rutland. All of the marble in this area was quarried from outcroppings, so the supply was not plentiful.[54] In 1821, Lyman Gray opened the Briggs Quarry, the second West Rutland marble site in addition to William Barnes's.[55] The Francis Slason Quarry opened in 1830 in West Rutland. It was worked for a short time, closed and then reopened a half-century later by the Standard Marble Company.

Early marble sites developed where the outcroppings were visible or very close to the surface. Vast deposits of valuable marble below the surface remained unsuspected. Development of the marble industry had achieved a modicum of success, but greater expansion awaited entrepreneurs with more vision who could tap these deposits.[56] Willard and Moses Humphrey of Sutherland Falls were among the first of the new entrepreneurs with this larger vision.

The Humphreys represented the most innovative of the early generation of marble producers. In the summer of 1836, the brothers became convinced that marble quarrying and sawing could be made more profitable. Seeing some of the success of the marble quarries in the west parish of Rutland, they decided to look for marble in the Sutherland Falls area of Rutland, downstream on the Otter Creek. A mile and a half south of the unincorporated village of Sutherland Falls, part of Rutland Town, the Humphreys found marble at a site later known as the Columbian Quarry. The Humphreys' quarry was the fourth quarry in Rutland and the first in Sutherland Falls (later renamed Proctor). The Humphreys' intuition of marble in the area was correct, but even they did not realize the full extent. The marble belt in Sutherland Falls was 1,650 to 2,200 feet wide.[57]

The Humphreys joined with Rutland lawyer Edgar L. Ormsbee under the firm name of Humphrey and Ormsbee and built a sawmill in the winter of 1836–37. It opened on September 26, 1837, with four gangs of saws to cut the marble into blocks for house foundations, fireplaces and gravestones.[58]

The firm was quite small, especially when compared to later standards, employing not more than five or six men. The Humphreys, however, began to expand the firm further. They opened a second site in the summer of 1838, known as the Sutherland Falls Quarry. The initial expense was quite high; when the financial crisis of 1837–38 hit, the Humphreys had little reserves to weather the financial storm. The panic of 1837 curtailed any expansion for most businesses in the area. The sense of hopelessness and financial doom hung in the air. The *Herald* noted in an editorial, "Integrity and talent add nothing…Surely this is a Dark Age! An Awful period in our political history. Where and how it will terminate God only knows."[59]

For the Humphreys, it was a financial disaster. Creditors forced them to liquidate their assets. The Humphrey firm was assigned to Francis Slason of West Rutland. Slason hired Moses Humphrey, now no longer an owner, to act as superintendent, but this attempt to save the company failed as well.

Under Slason's direction, the business struggled on another three or four years. Discouraged by the turn of events, the Humphrey brothers soon gave up all interest in the business and left the area.[60]

Though unsuccessful, the Humphreys' firm was a harbinger of changes to come in the 1840s. During that decade, the industry slowly shifted from individuals and small firms that dealt with one or two aspects of the business to marble companies that integrated quarrying, cutting, polishing, distribution and promotion.

After the Humphreys, the next outstanding entrepreneur of the marble industries was William F. Barnes, son of the early marble entrepreneur William Barnes. Barnes's business acumen became legendary. He began quarrying in 1839, employing three or four men on his land. In 1841, he discovered a vein of marble about a half-mile northeast of the old Blanchard quarry, lying on the western edge of the swamp, in the middle of what would become West Rutland, between Main and Pleasant Streets. In 1842, he bought another seven or eight acres for $335 and later more land for $3,000. In November 1844, he bought an additional five acres on the east side of the wetlands (on the Pleasant Street side) from the estate of Asa Hale. Through the years, he continued to buy more land and hire more workers.[61]

Barnes was entering the market at an auspicious time, when the transportation revolution would greatly transform the means of moving the bulky blocks of marble. Earlier attempts to improve transportation had achieved only minor success. As early as 1825, a River Canal had been approved for the Rutland area, but the cost and the engineering involved discouraged actual work on the project. Railroads offered another possibility, but construction did not begin on the Rutland and Burlington Railroad until 1847. In 1849, the railroad nosed its way down through the valley and reached Rutland, including its northern village of Sutherland Falls.[62]

Barnes was innovative in extracting as much valuable marble as possible. He invented a process that significantly changed marble production and was imitated by the rest of the industry. Instead of blasting the marble to free it, a process that damaged much of the block of marble, he reasoned that cutting the marble to loosen it would release most of the marble undamaged. His new channeling process would prove to be much more economical than the traditional method of blasting. Barnes had found a bed of marble consisting of slabs that had seams on three sides; however, on the fourth side the marble was secured to the bed. Drilling a channel along the fourth side allowed workers to release the marble slab. Barnes then began, on a regular basis, to use a long-churn drill to make cuts or channels across the marble in order to carve out large blocks.[63]

Barnes's inventiveness was shown in other ways, as well. He utilized the first derrick in the town, driven by horses or oxen, to lift the blocks of marble up the quarry side. Two or three years later, a steam engine replaced the animals and provided the energy to lift the marble.[64] At the surface, blocks were placed on a stone "boat" and then dragged to a mill for sawing. At the sawmill, a soft strip of iron, with no teeth, passed back and forth over the marble, driven by steam or water power. The strip wore its way through the marble because sand was thrown on the surface to act as an abrasive to grind down the stone; the constant interaction of the iron saw and the sand gradually split the rock. Gangs of saws, in a timber framework four to five feet wide and eight to twelve feet long, slowly sliced their way through the marble. The success of the steam engine in lifting the heavy marble blocks led to its use in other areas of the industry, as well. Steam engines began replacing hand channeling to lower labor expense and improve productivity.

In 1843, William F. Barnes joined with William Y. Ripley, from the prominent Ripley family of Rutland (and the father of the future Civil War generals William Y.W. Ripley and Edward H. Ripley), to form a marble company. Barnes and Ripley were business partners from 1843 to 1850. Together, Barnes and the senior Ripley built the Ripley Mill at Center Rutland. They eventually divided their properties, Ripley taking the mill at Center Rutland and Barnes, the quarries at West Rutland. Later, Ripley, along with his sons, would form a rival marble company, Ripley and Sons (the name was later changed to Ripley Sons after the death of the father).

With the advent of Charles Sheldon (1839) and W.Y. Ripley (1844), marble production became a more formalized industry. Sheldon was responsible for the large-scale opening of the West Rutland marble deposit, beginning in 1844 when he developed the quarry belonging to the company of Sheldon and Sons and Adams and Allen (later the quarry of Gilson and Woodfin).[65] Two years later, after the formation of Barnes and Ripley's company in 1845, Lorenzo Sheldon, Francis Slason and David Morgan set up a rival company. In 1848, the *Rutland Herald* began to carry advertisements for Davis, Morgan and Company, extolling in bombastic phrases the marble from "celebrated" West Rutland quarries. In 1850, teamsters transported 7,300 tons of marble from the West Rutland quarries to Whitehall, New York, at the cost of

Another postcard from the period offers a closer view of a quarry. It eventually reached an estimated depth of three hundred feet. *Courtesy of Vermont Marble Company.*

$30,650.[66] In 1850, Barnes, the largest employer in the area, had fifty men working for him, with an average monthly salary of $20.[67]

In July 1850, Barnes planned to erect two new marble sawing mills—one steam powered and the other water powered—to increase his output. In August 1850, Barnes acquired land and water rights at Gookin Falls, the second-largest falls on the Otter Creek, from William Gookin for $3,000. One month later, Baxter, Strong and Harrington transferred their rights in the operation to the Rutland Marble Company. By 1850, production of marble was surging. Pitt W. Hyde quarried 13,500 tons of marble that year. More marble was quarried in West Rutland than in any other town in Vermont, and probably in the world, in 1850; more varieties of marble were produced here than in any other single town in the state or the nation.[68] The 1857 *Report on the Geology of Vermont* indicated that 989 men were involved in quarrying and produced 3,063,240 feet of Vermont marble. If the marble had been sawed into slabs two inches thick, it would have covered more than seventy acres.

In 1853, William Barnes sold some of his quarries and mills to the Rutland Marble Company for $125,000.[69] Due to his business acumen, by 1854 Barnes employed 80 men and produced 300,000 feet of marble annually, making him one of the largest employers in the state.[70] Throughout the state, there were twenty-seven mills with 176 gangs of saws; the mills employed 312 men. Including all workers, the marble industry employed over 1,300 men in 1857; it was the largest single industry in the state other than farming.[71] The most common occupation, portrayed in an 1853 painting by James Hope of the old Sheldon, Slason & Morgan Quarry in West Rutland, was cutting the stone out of the quarry.

In 1854, the North River Mining Company purchased an old marble company in the area and employed sixty men as the demand for marble increased. The following year saw more reorganization at the quarry in Sutherland Falls, under the name of American Marble Company; most of the investors were from New York State. Former Rutland and Burlington Railroad superintendent John S. Dunlap became president and treasurer of American Marble Company. He soon reorganized it as Sutherland Falls Marble Company, and the continually expanding firm added Rutland attorney John Prouty and businessman John B. Page to its board of directors.[72]

H.H. Baxter, head of the Rutland Marble Company, planned for new quarries to open by the fall of 1854 and the winter of 1855. Already the old West Rutland quarry, known as the Barnes Quarry, had reached a depth of 100 feet and a length of 1,680 feet and had yielded 16 million cubic feet of marble. In 1855, the Rutland Marble Company employed 150 men, producing 400,000 feet of marble.[73]

West Rutland exemplifies the expansion taking place in the valley during the 1850s. In 1847, West Rutland had a Congregational church, three stores and twenty dwellings. The Rutland and Washington Railroad was completed in West Rutland in 1852, putting in place the infrastructure required to support the growth in the workforce. By 1857, there were 1,294 Irish Catholics living in the unincorporated village of West Rutland, most of them working in the burgeoning marble industry.[74]

While Barnes's operations were the largest, other firms contributed to the transformation of the valley into the Marble Valley. In Brandon, C.P. Austin and E.D. Selden operated quarries. In Wallingford, J. Adair and Brother and General Robinson Hall each had a quarry, and Anson Warner had a quarry in South Wallingford.

This group of laborers in West Rutland demonstrates the predominance of Irish laborers in Vermont Marble's early years, judging by their surnames. All but one came from Eire. The lone non-Irish surname, Anderson, stems from Scandinavia. *Courtesy of Rutland Historical Society.*

Sutherland Falls Marble Company operated in Sutherland Falls. The largest concentration of quarries was in West Rutland. In addition to the Rutland Marble Company, quarries were operated by Adams and Allen; Sheldon and Slason; Sherman, Holley and Adams; the Vermont Marble Company; and the Hydeville Company. Farther south, the next concentration of quarries was located around Danby, with companies run by W.W. Kelley and Thomas Syminton; R.P. Bloomer and Clark and Folsom; M. and G.B. Holley; and, in Dorset Way, Wilson Sanford and Company. East Dorset had three working quarries: Firedly, McDonald & Holley and Fields & Kent.[75]

The high return on investment spurred growth throughout the Vermont Marble Valley. Based on the 1850 Industrial Census, and looking on the rate of return after subtracting labor costs and start-up costs, lucrative returns were possible. Later in the century, with a wider distribution network and more effective marble industry controls on the price of the product, even greater returns could be achieved. Protective tariffs would also shield the domestic marble industry from foreign competition.

Sheldon, Morgan and Slason led producers in 1850 with a 308 percent investment return. The Hydeville Company, just west of Rutland near

Castleton, was a close second with a 307 percent return. William P. Elliot had a 95 percent return. William F. Barnes, an early marble leader, had a 73 percent return. Some of the marble leaders more than recouped their investments in one year. It was this financial return that attracted emerging social and political leaders.

Entrepreneurs could only realize these profits by tapping an abundant labor force. This, too, was now available. The potato famine in Ireland led many Irish to immigrate to the United States, finding work in the construction of railroads and working in mines and quarries. The earlier generation of white Anglo-Saxon Protestant settlers was now in a position to develop the quarrying and mineral rights to the land. Railroads made it easier to transport the bulky material to national markets, where the stone could receive a better price. The combined benefits of transportation, an increased workforce and marketing created the opportunity for a high return on investment.

In later years, the *Rutland Daily Herald*, impressed with the wealth coming from the marble quarries, commented on the growth in the valley:

> As far back as 1835 the white quarries of Vermont were uncovered, but not until ten years ago [1870] did they loom up to claim a place among the ambitious industries of America. Forty years ago [1840] no prospect favored, and every obstacle hindered any extensive development of these Green Mountain mines of wealth. But when the demand was loud enough to be heard among these hills, the marble rose from its sepulcher of ages and marched from the mountains to market.[76]

These were "mines of wealth"—not quarries, but *mines*, conjuring up images of vast and traditional wealth associated with gold and silver mines.

The marble wealth of the 1850s effected the dramatic growth in real estate in the next decade. The *Rutland Daily Herald* for December 23, 1872, commented on the spectacular growth of real estate values in Rutland that had followed in the 1860s:

> An exchange says: Land which was sold in Springfield, Massachusetts for $250 an acre ten years ago has just been bought back by the same parties for $8,000 an acre. What of it? Land that went a-begging, twenty-five years ago in Rutland for seventy-five to a hundred dollars an acre could not be bought now for thirty thousand.[77]

The real estate boom had an impact on the workers coming to the Marble Valley. The many small marble companies that had acquired land before the dramatic increase in real estate values could now derive added revenue from company houses that they rented to their workers. Many standardized duplex side-by-side houses were built close together so as not to waste space. Since land and houses were comparatively expensive, the owners could use housing as leverage against any worker strike or disturbance. In the 1860s, the owners used this means to quash strikes in the marble industry. Workers now faced a lock-out from their housing and also their work. Such an arrangement gave increased power to the marble owners.

The engine of the new wealth was the marble industry and the workers it attracted. In the 1860s and 1870s, this expansion continued. In 1860, there were more than fifty quarries throughout the state, most of them clustered around Rutland.[78] Throughout the 1860s, the marble workers and the marble elites were instrumental in Rutland's growth. With the economic, social and, later, political influence of the marble industry and the vital transportation

An early three-bay mill bears the name Sutherland Falls. It opened circa 1836–37 and was eventually part of the consolidation that formed the base of the early Vermont Marble Company. *Courtesy of Rutland Historical Society.*

link of the railroads, Rutland overtook its rival, Burlington, as the largest city in the state, with a population of twelve thousand by 1880.[79]

In the 1850s, railroad construction had brought additional workers into the area, especially immigrants who settled in the area and worked the quarries. The dramatic expansion of the railroads in the 1860s and 1870s provided the important infrastructure essential for transporting and distribution bulky materials such as marble.

The earlier canal—and, more importantly, the railroad—allowed marble companies to develop external distribution centers at a time when the highly compressed calcium carbonate was a social statement of wealth and opulence. In an age of conspicuous consumption, marble conferred historical and social status. Marble was a feature in the humble forty-room "cottages" of Newport, Rhode Island. What was needed was someone who had the talent and ability to organize the industry. In the decade to come, Redfield Proctor would emerge as the most successful of the marble entrepreneurs.

CHAPTER 3

BECOMING KING
OF THE HILL

Redfield Proctor and the Marble Valley

Redfield Proctor, born in Proctorsville, Vermont, in 1831, was part of a remarkable generation of new business leaders who were born between 1830 and 1845. As young men between the ages of fifteen and thirty, they faced a common set of economic, social, political, intellectual and religious situations that shaped their thinking, attitudes and behavior.[80] The most important of these, of course, was the Civil War. It forced this generation to deal with the logistics of supply and distribution of men and supplies for a massive conflict, learning lessons that later could be translated into building an industry to supply a mass market. Throughout the Marble Valley, you will notice the influence of Redfield Proctor.

His social, political, business and organizational skills, derived from the recent war, aided in his social and political rise. He began this political ascent in conjunction with his law practice shortly after he arrived in Rutland, serving as Rutland's representative to the Vermont House of Representatives. In 1868, he left politics for six years while he concentrated on organizing and building his newly acquired marble business.

In 1874, he reentered politics as state senator from Rutland County. As senator, he was elected president *pro tempore* by his fellow senators and chaired the powerful Senate Rules Committee. In 1874, he introduced legislation to set limits on maximum rates for the transportation of marble, although it failed in committee due to the influential lobbying by railroads. In 1876, he became lieutenant governor and secured the 1878 Republican nomination for governor. He was elected governor that year and served until 1880.[81]

This Italianate-style home served as Redfield Proctor's Rutland Village home before he moved his family to the lowlands near the Proctor Depot and the Vermont Marble Company finishing mill. *Mike Austin Collection.*

Rutland was a growing commercial center with a larger population that provided Proctor with more financial opportunities than Proctorsville. After the Civil War, rather than starting off by himself and having to develop a practice, he shrewdly entered into a legal partnership with Wheelock G. Veazey, a comrade from the war. Veazey; Walter C. Dunton, another former soldier; and Proctor formed the partnership[82] Proctor, Veazey and Dunton at 9 Merchants Row.[83]

To signify his new social and financial status, Proctor built a dignified Italianate-style house at the corner of 1 Field Avenue and Grove Street, still occupied today, and lived there until 1871. In an article concerning the dramatic expenditures in new construction taking place in Rutland after the war, the *Rutland Daily Herald* noted specifically Redfield Proctor's new Grove Street house:

> *Total outlay in building for the year was $240,000. The great stride made by our prosperous village during the year 1867, in its onward march is almost incomprehensible to our inhabitants who are here and can see for*

Blocks of marble, cut into uniform sizes, await further modification or shipment. *Courtesy of Vermont Marble Museum.*

themselves, while to those at a distance, who have been eyewitnesses of our progress, the story of such rapid improvements within the period mentioned is almost too great to be believed...Redfield Proctor's house is [valued at] *$10,000.*[84]

Marble companies were the source of much of the prosperity coming to Rutland. The *Rutland Herald* commented on the financial returns possible and contrasted some of the other companies to the faltering Sutherland Falls Marble Company.[85] The Rutland Marble Company, for instance, was established in the year 1867 with assets of $41,506.91, with stockholders receiving dividends of $75,000.00 during the year. The net return for the year was a sizeable 14 percent.[86]

When the failure of financial speculators, including Jay Gould and James Fisk, touched off a panic on the infamous Black Friday of September 24, 1869, Sutherland Falls Marble Company was in no position to endure the financial storm and was forced into receivership by its creditors. About November 10, 1869, Redfield Proctor set out from his law office on

Postcards from the 1880s depicted the Vermont Marble Company quarry in a community that had already changed its name to Proctor (1886). *Courtesy of Vermont Marble Company.*

Merchants Row for the northwest section of Rutland, known as Sutherland Falls, to deal with the financial and business interests of Dorr and Myers. Dorr and Myers had overexpanded in the 1860s. The court had appointed Proctor as the company's receiver until the situation could be resolved.

A short distance from Dorr and Myers, and next to the railroad, was the larger Sutherland Falls Marble Company (privately owned primarily by Massachusetts investors). Proctor saw the advantage of combining Dorr and Myers with Sutherland Falls Marble Company, utilizing the four natural resources that the area provided at the falls: power from the Otter Creek; an existing profitable, proven quarry; a favorable terrain such that blocks could easily be lowered by the force of gravity to a nearby mill; and a good supply of marble-sawing sand between the mill and the quarry. In 1869, the Sutherland Falls Marble Company had installed a track running from its mill to the quarries.

In November 1870, one year after Proctor was appointed receiver, he reorganized the two companies, Dorr and Myers plus the original Sutherland Falls Marble Company, into the second Sutherland Falls Marble Company. Instead of being controlled from out of state, as the first had been by Massachusetts-based interests, the new Sutherland Falls Marble Company was a Vermont company, with Proctor as the largest stockholder. In the spring of 1871, Proctor moved his family from his $10,000 home on Grove Street in Rutland to a new house in Sutherland Falls north of Main Street on the west side of the Great Falls, where the present-day park is located in Proctor.[87] In his concern for effective management, Proctor could be closer to the company, focus on its concerns and begin his own rise to become the biggest marble magnate of all.

One month after Proctor arrived in Sutherland Falls, a tragic event took place in West Rutland that symbolized the transition of marble leadership from one generation to another: one of the early titans of the marble industry, William F. Barnes, was crushed to death by a large block of marble.[88] Barnes had been one of the old guard—a sympathetic, kindly and shrewd man who was compassionate to his workers and also, like Proctor, had a sense of the importance of organization. Unlike Proctor, however, he had lacked the legal, organizational and political skills and connections so necessary after the Civil War.[89]

One of the dangers that the domestic marble industry faced was imported marble. As late as 1870, the amount of marble imported into the United States from Italy exceeded Vermont's marble production. Proctor and other marble producers were concerned, and for Proctor, the solution was obvious and apparent. He began to lobby for a protective tariff for marble.[90] The close connection of Republican politics and business meant that politics—Republican politics—could be used to further domestic business interests.

There were domestic dangers in addition to foreign competition. A short time after he took over, Proctor faced an economic recession. The Great Panic that began in 1873 and lasted until 1878 caught workers in an economic squeeze, but for those with capital, however modest, it provided an opportunity. Here Proctor's luck held once more. Coming into the market with sufficient capital in the 1860s or early 1870s before the panic, he saw the time as one of great opportunities. Proctor could see the potential for return in the marble industry and was willing to defer the returns. He also was willing to risk his own money on that return. Proctor invested all the money he had in the new Sutherland Falls Marble Company, becoming its treasurer and overall manager.[91]

Proctor sought to expand his market. Branch offices would allow the company to enter strategically into the rapidly growing Midwest. Consequently, he established the first branch of the Sutherland Falls Marble Company outside New England at Toledo, Ohio, in 1875, with Henry D.

Pierce as manager. Like Proctor, Pierce had been at first an outsider to the marble business, but he had the organizational skills that Proctor valued, and he gave up teaching as a career to go into the marble business, first in Toledo and later in the larger Chicago market.

Proctor needed to secure eastern markets as well. Boston, Philadelphia and the large New York market were the most important. By 1878, branch distributing offices were in place in both Boston and Toledo, and Proctor established outlets in New York, Philadelphia, Chicago and San Francisco.[92]

Proctor also began to expand the company's product line to include monument finishing (1876) and exterior finishing (1880). About 1876, the Sutherland Falls Marble Company added another step to the manufacturing process by finishing the marble it sawed.[93] By 1880, the finishing section of the Sutherland Falls Company had expanded to three rubbing beds and thirty lathes. At first, the finishing was used only for monumental work, but later it was expanded to include exterior building products such as door caps, lintels, facing and solid walls.

As the nation recovered from the depression of the late 1870s, it went on a building spree. On January 12, 1880, the *Rutland Herald* commented on the impact for Vermont and Rutland; the economic forecast described the new developments as a divine providence unfolding:

> *America had to become great before she could utilize her great resources. With each epoch of enlargement has come to light some new fountain of wealth which that epoch alone could open. As man has multiplied his own facilities, nature has responded in larger ratios and furnished inexhaustible incentives to his ingenuity and skill. When our architecture was ready for marble, then marble was uncovered, quarried, and supplied. As architecture approached elegance, and as increased prosperity enabled the popular taste to respond to the allurements of luxury, marble as a material for building and ornamentation, attained to a pronounced demand. But Italy, with its pauper-wretched labor, was ready to supply the demand at prices, which defied any home competition. Further, the extent, value, durability and availability of Vermont marble was unknown abroad and unappreciated at home.[94]*

The number of people involved in the marble industry "in and around Rutland is seen in the nearly 2,000 hands employed in the more than 200 gangs of saws running day and night, in nearly 60,000 tons of marble shipped annually."[95]

Later that month, the *Herald* reported the election of Redfield Proctor to the presidency of the Rutland Marble Company at the annual meeting of that company held in New York. The *Herald* went on to report:

> *It is well known that on account of the hard times and the very sharp competition, none of the marble interests in Vermont have been, for two or three years, at least, in a flourishing condition. This is especially true of the West Rutland or white marble trade. It is well known that Mr. Baxter for some years wished to be relieved of the care of the management of the Rutland Marble company to enable him to devote more time to the bank and his other important business interests, and tendered his resignation some months ago, but did not insist on its acceptance until the company could make other satisfactory arrangements…*
>
> *Gov. Proctor, as president, will take over the active management of the affairs at West and Center Rutland, and Salem, N.Y. No other changes in the employees or the officers of the company is expected. The change was not brought about by any hostile movement, but has been entirely harmonious and unanimous on the part of the stockholders and directors…*
>
> *As the two companies (Sutherland Falls and Rutland Marble companies) employ 1,000 or more men, when running full, and have properties capable of almost infinite development, with their large water power and quarries, the change is a very important one, and we think must prove beneficial.*[96]

This report marked a new and powerful business combination. In 1880, at the end of ten years of Proctor's management, the number of workers at Sutherland Falls Marble Company at Sutherland Falls had risen to three hundred, operating sixty-four gangs and producing 94,500 cubic feet of marble, worth $225,000. In the summer of 1880, the company completed its first shop to produce large building exteriors, one hundred feet long and fifty-six feet wide. The first large building exterior cut in Proctor (for the Indianapolis, Indiana State Capitol) was produced in the shop in 1881. It included seventy-two polished marble columns thirteen feet high and two feet four inches in diameter.[97]

By 1880, the Rutland Marble Company had—besides its quarries at West Rutland, which covered the largest holding on the West Rutland deposit—twenty-four gangs at West Rutland, twenty-eight gangs at Center Rutland and eight gangs at Salem, New York, for a total of sixty gangs. It employed more than 450 men but had never prospered.[98]

In 1880, Proctor became involved with Rutland Marble Company. He happened to be in New York City, visiting a friend's office, when Elisha Riggs, a New York banker and president of the Rutland Marble Company, stepped into the room. Riggs and Proctor, who knew of each other but had not met previously, were formally introduced. Riggs, very much aware of the success of the Sutherland Falls Marble Company and the lack of success of his own Rutland Marble Company, proposed a deal to Proctor. The Rutland Marble Company, Riggs felt, was valuable property but was not succeeding because of mismanagement. Despite its name as the Rutland Marble Company, which gave the appearance that it was locally owned and run, investors from New York City owned the business and were more interested in immediate profits than in long-range development. The company felt compelled to hold auctions frequently to sell off marble to generate capital for the investors. The company had also overextended itself with a debt of $500,000 and had resorted to borrowing to pay dividends.[99]

Riggs proposed that Proctor assume the management of Rutland Marble. Like the original Sutherland Falls Company, Rutland Marble had expanded too rapidly and exceeded its revenues. By contrast, the current Sutherland Falls Marble Company, under Proctor, was free of debt and profitable. Riggs proposed that Proctor take over the hemorrhaging Rutland Marble Company and replace him as president of Rutland Marble. The same day, a meeting was quickly convened; Proctor returned to Vermont that night as president of Rutland Marble Company, with potentially lucrative operations in the West Rutland quarries. As president, Proctor received a salary of $1,000 a month and owned the largest amount of stock, with eight thousand shares, making him the largest stockholder with 27 percent of the stock and giving him virtual control of the company.[100]

Moving quickly, in September 1880 Proctor formed the Vermont Marble Company, which took over the property of both the Sutherland Falls Marble Company and the Rutland Marble Company.[101] This gave Proctor control of 55 percent of the marble trade in the Rutland region. Unlike the Rutland Marble Company and the first Sutherland Falls Marble Company, the new Vermont Marble Company was truly based in Vermont, locally owned and locally controlled. The combined company included 750 employees, making it by far the largest employer in the area. By 1889, the last year of Redfield Proctor's direct daily control of the company, it would grow to 1,400 workers, and in 1903 it would be the largest marble company in the world.[102]

Proctor formally announced the new company on January 1, 1881, when he advertised bonds of Vermont Marble in the *Rutland Herald*. The inducement stated:

> *Over $300,000 of these bonds have been sold in the last fifty days. Only $100,000 more will be offered for sale at par. Denominations of $100, $500, and $1000. Registered or coupon interest at five per cent. Principal interest payable in gold. A perfectly safe investment. For further information apply to either of the undersigned.*[103]

After becoming president of the new, larger company, Proctor now shifted his sights to another problem. To bring in operating capital, some marble companies had been hosting marble auctions, which drove down the prices that dealers would pay for marble. Proctor's competitors—particularly his chief rival, the Rutland Marble Company—often had held auctions at their quarries. Such a procedure had immediate advantages in raising cash but in the long run was disastrous. Proctor saw the need to wrest control from the buyer-distributor and give it to the producer-seller. His objective was to bring together the elements of the marble industry under one sales organization, reducing duplication and providing more effective control. Like Rockefeller in oil, he sought a mechanism that would combine the marble producers into a cartel to control the market.

In 1880, Proctor laid the groundwork to establish an alliance of the marble producers. A complimentary dinner was arranged to invite the principal producers to explore more cooperative strategies.[104] Proctor led the way in forming the Producers' Marble Company, a confederation of companies whose sole purpose was to control the price and distribution of marble; the participating companies were Vermont Marble Company; Gilson and Woodfin; Sheldon and Slason; Sherman and Gleason; and Ripley Sons, which owned a mill but no quarry. The *Rutland Herald* reported on the new company's formation:

> *Yesterday a meeting was held, lasting late into the night, at the Rutland County National Bank rooms, of all the Vermont marble producers, to*

consider matters of common interest…An organization was effected, called the "Vermont Marble Dealers Association." They made choice of W.Y.W. Ripley, President; Chas. Sheldon, Vice-President; Ed. H. Ripley, Secretary; Redfield Proctor, E.P. Gilson, H.G. Root, Rockwood Barrett, Wyman Flint, executive committee. They hope to accomplish, not only good for themselves, but for their customers by securing greater uniformity of prices and refusing credit to irresponsible parties who have done great injury to the trade by underselling legitimate dealers throughout the country, and restore this great industry to its former prosperity.

There will be a slight advance in prices—less than ten per cent—which is less than the increased cost of production. It is also proposed to cut off the system of indiscriminate discounts which has prevailed of late, and has been so unequal and unjust in its operations.[105]

As they pooled their sales, yards and closer cooperation began showing effects; the Rutland-based group took on the name of the Producers' Marble Company. Competition in producing marble was to be avoided, especially among the members of the cartel. To ensure that no member undercut the price of another, Proctor devised spheres of influence with exclusive control. For example, the Boston branch of the Producers' Marble Company had exclusive rights to sell marble from the Connecticut River east and into the Maritime Provinces of Canada. No other member of the cartel could sell in that territory. The same model persisted throughout his distribution network. Thus, if a consumer wanted marble, he had to deal with the existing price, either nearby or in another region where the price would be maintained.

In 1883, Vermont Marble Company had 54.72 percent of the market controlled by the cartel. Its next nearest competitor was Sheldon and Sons with 23.8 percent; the other members and their percentages were Ripley Sons, 7.25 percent; Gilson and Woodfin, 7.0 percent; and Dorset Marble, 5.9 percent.[106] These five companies composed the Producers' Marble Company, which, in turn, controlled the national market. The new cartel was a façade—a voluntary, self-enforcing organization rather than an actual company, like a holding company; nevertheless, this pool controlled nearly 85 percent of the marble in Rutland County.[107]

Now that the price of marble could be maintained, Proctor turned to the distribution problem. The Vermont Marble Company increased its distribution points from four in 1881 to nine in 1886: Boston, New York, Philadelphia, Toledo, St. Louis, Chicago, Cleveland, Detroit and San Francisco. The principal branches were at Boston, Philadelphia and Chicago.[108] By 1888, the number had risen to eleven, with new branches in the Midwest at Cincinnati and Kansas City. Later, after the demise of the cartel, the Vermont Marble Company consolidated the branches, so the number dwindled from eleven to six.

In 1882, Proctor sought to formalize his international business power by being appointed to the U.S. Tariff Commission so that he could influence tariffs on imported marble. Appearing before the Tariff Commission as representative of more than a dozen marble companies, he asserted that businesses and employees, rather than being financially hurt, benefited from protectionism. The American worker needed protection from "the cheapest labor in the world," he said.[109] Throughout the 1880s, he maintained his protectionist position. Government connections at all levels—local, state and national—might enhance business connections. To add more political pressure, he sought alliances with Georgia's developing marble industry to jointly lobby against foreign competition. Meanwhile, in addition to the stock he owned in his company, he also purchased its bonds so that, by 1882, he owned $250,000 worth of stocks and bonds in the Vermont Marble Company.[110]

Proctor also sought to deal with foreign competition head-on. Northern Italy was a center of the Italian marble industry, from which marble was shipped to the United States. Up until 1870, more Italian marble was imported into the United States than was quarried in Vermont. He traveled to Carrara, the heart of the marble industry of Italy, to lure away the best carvers and bring them to work for his company in Vermont and to force the replacement of an American consul in Carrara with a man who would promote Vermont Marble Company interests.

After concluding that the current American consul was not acting in the best interests of the American marble companies, he organized other Vermont producers in support of Charles Bernard, already a U.S. consul to northern Italy but not stationed in the marble area. Bernard was a Rutlander whose father-in-law was E.P. Gilson, one of the owners of the Gilson and Woodfin Marble Company of Rutland. Because of his marble and Vermont connections, Bernard could be relied on to represent the New England marble producers' interests.

With Proctor's political and business connections, Bernard was soon the new U.S. consul. The following year, Proctor used his influence to secure the appointment of Ulisse Boccacci, an Italian, who sought the position of agent for Consul Bernard. Boccacci, "in this old boy network," did receive the appointment and felt obligated to Proctor.[111] The combination promotion of Vermont marble at home and restriction of marble from Italy would increase domestic sales.

While in Italy, Proctor availed himself of the opportunity to recruit highly skilled Italian stonecutters and sculptors, persuading them to come to Vermont. He also added to his product line Italian marble, but this was always a minor part of the business. As a marketing strategy, he wanted access to this market of skilled, world-renowned carvers and persuaded eighteen skilled stonecutters to come to Proctor. These northern Italians, so-called Alta Italians, arrived in 1881, followed by another group who arrived in 1885.[112] All of the northern Italians who came to Proctor were skilled craftsmen, stonecutters or marble carvers.[113]

As Proctor continued expanding his marble company, the *Rutland Herald* noted dramatic changes taking place in the Marble Valley and especially at Sutherland Falls, the headquarters of the Vermont Marble Company:

There are few places in the State that show the march of progress as much as Sutherland Falls. On every hand additions, and alternations are being made which greatly improve the efficiency and appearance of the marble works. The winter marble trade is usually light in comparison with the spring business, and the Vermont Marble Company has taken advantage of it by stocking their yard with first class blocks sawed to a desirable thickness, so they can be furnished promptly in sizes to suit customers when the busy season arrives…The work on the Indiana State House contract requires very heavy machinery and extra long gangs…A floor has been laid and a partition built in the finish building for the completing of the columns and pilasters. Although the company has a large sand bank near the store, they have purchased land on the east side of Otter Creek which bids fair to increase their excellent supply of sand. At the quarry the same activity is exhibited at the mills. Extra machinery is at work boring and cutting out the great blocks for the State House…The energy shown to bring about these improvements in the middle of winter is highly commendable.[114]

To lower transportation costs, the Vermont Marble Company on September 10, 1885, officially incorporated and organized the Clarendon and Pittsford Railroad, which operated from Florence at its north end and the Loveland quarry in Proctor (the new village created around the area known as Sutherland Falls), to Center Rutland and West Rutland, a total of seven and a half miles with the sidings. The railroad, wholly owned by the company, provided Proctor with another means of control. Between 1886 and 1890, the railroad was built in segments, connecting new quarries to the railroad.

Begun south from Proctor in 1886 and running to Center Rutland, the small line reached West Rutland in 1887 and 1888, thus conveniently uniting the main Proctor and West Rutland properties. Its primary business was transporting marble from the quarries to the company's huge, far-flung finishing mills; to increase revenues, it had the subsidiary goal of serving several private industries located along its right of way. The third biennial report of the Board of Railroad Commissioners for June 20, 1888, to June 30, 1890, had high praise for the Clarendon and Pittsford's construction: "It is a well built road and in every way equipped for the heavy traffic required, which is mainly the marble of the great quarries it was made to reach."[115]

In all, between 1885 and 1890, five major railroads serviced the Rutland area, helping to make it a center of activity. The Bennington and Rutland, Central Vermont, Clarendon and Pittsford, Delaware and Hudson and the Pittsford and Rutland provided vital transportation that helped the growth of the marble industry and the region.

Rutland, through the influence of Proctor and others, had become a center of the marble industry not only in New England but also nationally. The *Rutland Herald* announced an important meeting of marble dealers to be held in Rutland. "Marble Princes To Make Their Pilgrimage to the Mecca of the Trade Today" headlined the paper in its July 24, 1888 edition. Two days later, the *Herald* announced another indication of the economic and political influence of the Marble Valley. It headlined "Marble Dealers Association Selects State Officers." Notices had been sent to 475 dealers throughout New England and the nearby Canadian provinces.

In 1887, the Vermont Marble Company was strong enough to control the market directly, and at that point the Producers' Marble Company was dissolved. Proctor also sought measures of stability and control for the marble that he would import from Italy. In 1889, the Vermont Marble Company

Redfield Proctor's home in the town of Proctor welcomed President William Henry Harrison in 1891. A close look at the Oriental-style decorations hints that guests were celebrating the opening of trade with the Far East. *Courtesy of Rutland Historical Society.*

Vice-President Theodore Roosevelt was another guest at the Redfield Proctor home. He was vacationing in Vermont when the Secret Service reached him with news that President William McKinley had been shot. *Courtesy of Rutland Historical Society.*

A historic sign at the site of the Vermont Marble Company indicating that it was the largest marble company in the world. Many of the Vermont Marble Company buildings are still located in Proctor and are being used by the Vermont Marble Museum and the OMYA Marble Company, the successor to the Vermont Marble Company. *Mike Austin Collection.*

purchased a quarter interest in a sailing ship to bring Italian marble to its San Francisco branch. The company acquired a thirty-year lease on the Sheldon Marble Company of West Rutland in 1891. Thus, by 1891, the Vermont Marble Company had either acquired outright or taken control of all of its former associates in the Vermont Marble Dealers pool. By 1891, the Vermont Marble Company had reached a pinnacle that no other marble company in the United States had achieved. When it absorbed former cartel members Ripley Sons and Gilson and Woodfin, it became the largest marble company in the country, with 1,800 workers in 1894, and by the turn of the century, it had become the largest in the world.[116]

Internally and externally, Proctor had made his company successful. Redfield Proctor had become "King of the Valley." By forming the Vermont Marble Company and successfully leading it through the 1880s, he was catapulted financially to the top of the social and political elite of the town. As a former governor, he ran socially in a circle that included former governor John B. Page, Charles Clement and the Ripley brothers, all members of a marble elite who had stately mansions in the area. He was now unquestionably the king of the hill. The valley in which he had acquired his fortune and political fame also achieved a special identity. Marble mills ran all day and into the night. Trains ran several times a day, transporting the marble to distant places and belching steam and smog into the air. To the residents, this was the Marble Valley, and quarries were part of the changed landscape. Production of marble had made for a new economic lord but in an industry that demanded from its laborers hard work and often long hours.

CHAPTER 4

FROM THE QUARRIES
TO THE MILL

The Workers and the Work

Work in the quarries was ancillary to farming, and workers came from eastern and southern New England and nearby New York into the valley. Just before mid-century, the Irish immigrated in large numbers, followed by the French from Canada and the Welsh. By the end of the nineteenth century, other nationalities, especially Scandinavians, Italians and lastly Poles—as many as twenty at one time or another—worked in the marble industry.

During its rapid expansion, the industry had a constant demand for workers; marble companies sought young men. "Young Men," the Sutherland Falls Company advertised, "of good mechanical ability wanted at once to learn to turn marble. Fair wages to begin with and good prospect of advancement. Sutherland Falls Marble Co., Sutherland Falls."[117] The entry level for work in the quarries was about age fourteen; the exit level was about eighty or death. Age fourteen was a common age in the nineteenth century for young men to leave school and enter the workforce to support their families; earlier than that was unusual. At the quarries, children ages ten to fourteen, might be water-boys or translators, employed to bring water to the workers on a hot day or to translate the foremen's instructions to immigrant workers, respectively.[118]

With no adequate retirement plan for the average worker, old age meant work or financial support from the younger members of the family. Because there was such demand, some older workers continued to work at arduous tasks. Quarryman George Hadley, for instance, was seventy in 1880. John

Sweeney, John McCue, Thomas Welch and Peter Gaffney, all of them born in Ireland and in their late sixties, were still considered active quarrymen that year. Even Patrick Coffee, seventy-six, was considered a quarryman. The oldest person still working in the marble business in 1880 was Francis Slason, ninety, who described himself as a "capitalist."[119] He was a partner at an important marble company.

Immigrant families tended to be larger than those of Yankee origin and often reflected the geographic mobility of the families' wanderings. John Loso, born in Canada like his mother and father, came from a family of seven. John Lahway was born in Vermont, but his father was born in Canada and his mother in Ireland; John was also part of a seven-member household.

Of the eleven families in the 1880 Census sample that number ten or more, nine are Irish and two are Canadian. Patrick Garvin, whose parents were born in Ireland, came from a family of ten. Michael Clifford, born in Vermont of Irish parents, came from a family of fourteen. Michael Hackett, forty-eight and born in Ireland of Irish parents, was listed as being part of a family of twelve. Samuel Leonard, forty-seven and born in Canada of Canadian parents, had an eleven-member family. So did Hugh Clark, thirty-eight, himself born in Ireland of Irish parents. Edward McConnic, forty, likewise born in Ireland of Irish parents, was another eleven-member family man, and so was John Penders.

Although young men began working in the quarries, the largest number of workers in the 1880 Census sample were age thirty to fifty, in the same generation as (or the next younger one than) founder Redfield Proctor, who was forty-nine in 1880. In any given age group over thirty, the largest numbers of workers were nearly always Irish; in the under-thirty set, they were second-generation Irish.

Because of prejudice and tradition, some ethnic groups were informally restricted to certain types of jobs in the marble industry. Family members would often work in the same sector of the industry—for example, in the quarries or in office work. The Irish in the 1850s and 1860s were generally confined to the quarries and did not achieve management positions in proportion to their numbers.

By 1870, there were more opportunities for individuals from various ethnic groups, including the newly arrived Swedes. Swedes worked in all branches of the marble business in Proctor: Charles Larson worked in the quarry, John Ball worked in the mill, Erick Lundquist was a grader, John

Aronson worked at the rubbing bed, William Oberg was a stonecutter, Charles Johnson was a hand polisher and Emile Freden was a machine polisher. Other Swedes boxed finished marble pieces, worked in shipping or were engineers or draftsmen. Swedes were recruited to Vermont because they were viewed as dependable.[120] The Rutland Marble Company in 1871 employed nearly one hundred Swedes, who were "described as being very active, industrious, and quiet men."[121] Several members of the board of managers were Swedes, and Fred Aronson, a Swede, was a member of the board of directors in 1880.[122]

One Swede recalls the long hours and the pay. "We were not poor—we were just *awfully* poor. Dad worked 72 hours a week for $10.08. There was seldom any take-home pay. It was invariably traded out at the company store. We all worked at whatever we could find to do to earn a little money. Prices were low, but money also was very scarce. If I remember correctly, house rent, a ton of coal and a barrel of flour were about the same price—$3.75."[123]

The 1870s expansion of the marble industry drew more workers. The tremendous growth of labor in the next two decades made an impact on everyone in the region.

The 1880 Census reflected the growth of the marble industry and the diversity of the worker skills needed. The predominant immigrant groups in the 1880 Census were Irish and French Canadians. Some Scandinavians had started to arrive. Getting skilled workers was a growing problem in the 1870s and 1880s. When Redfield Proctor went to Italy to deal with restrictions on Italian marble, he also recruited premier experienced Italian workers from the marble district of northern Italy. Dante Bacolli and A. Fabiani were the first Italian cutters to work in Proctor.[124]

Most of the Italians living in Sutherland Falls (later Proctor) came from northern Italy and were literate, highly skilled carvers, sculptors and cutters, actively recruited initially by Proctor himself from the prestigious Italian marble district of Carrara. The immigrants paid for their own passage or were reimbursed by the company once they had arrived in the town of Proctor. Paying $11.00 board per month, they earned wages from $1.25 to $3.00 per day, dependent upon skill and experience.[125] Barre, the center of the granite industry, also attracted an Italian community. Like Proctor's recruitment of skilled carvers, the Italians in Barre were also skilled. Writing in 1913 about Italians who had come to Barre, Arthur Brayley noted:

The Italian Aid Society in Center Rutland is one of the two Italian social/support groups formed by early immigrant groups. Among its many functions, it offered bulk buying of specialty food ingredients. In Rutland, there were two Italian clubs, indicating a cultural division between northern and southern Italians. *Courtesy of Rutland Historical Society.*

The Italian American Club in Rutland City forms the other nucleus for Italian American heritage activities. *Mike Austin Collection.*

About one-half of the population of the city are Italians; not of the class that comes from Italy by the thousand to make the roadbeds and dig the ditches of America, but men from the northern part of the country, skilled workmen, who have transferred their field of labor from the fine marble of Italy to the harder granite of Vermont. Among them are some of the best sculptors and their work is admired all over the United States, in fact wherever monuments of Barre granite are seen.[126]

The same divisions in social status that Brayley observed in Barre occurred in Rutland. The northern, Alta Italians established on February 12, 1894, the Italian Aid Society with a building that also served as a club. The land was donated to the society by the Vermont Marble Company. Other Italians from the south of Italy had a separate club located near the business district downtown on Grove Street.[127] Immigrants from southern Italy most often found work in the maintenance department of the railroad or in other large businesses. Some set up grocery stores in the ethnic neighborhood near St. Peter's Church on Convent Avenue. Between 1880 and 1920, there were representatives of as many as twenty nationalities living in Proctor alone.[128]

There were two peak waves of immigrants from Sweden, one in 1882 and another in 1890. The Swedes—northern European, light-skinned and Protestant—were looked upon most favorably. The *Commissioner's Report on Manufacturing and Agriculture* of 1890 reflected an affirmative attitude toward the Swedes. The report stated in part:

For many years the Commissioner has traveled extensively through the Western States, and watched their development, making note of the people of various nationalities on the broad prairies. His attention has been called to the thrifty, hard-working, honest Scandinavian, especially from Sweden. This class of immigrants came from a country resembling Vermont in soil, vegetation, configuration of surface and nature of climate, although the last is much more rigorous in Sweden than in Vermont. They are well educated, and hasten to have their children attend school where only English is spoken. They readily and quickly assimilate with our people, and become Americanized sooner than any other class of immigrant. They are temperate in their habits, and are religiously inclined…peaceful, mind their own business, pay their debts and are never objects of public charity.[129]

Poles, the last of the major immigrant groups to come to Rutland, arrived in West Rutland in the 1880s from Pennsylvania, when the quarries in that region had a slump. In the years between 1888 and 1890, the marble companies brought Polish immigrants from New York City to West Rutland, and their descendants are still there today. Nearly all of the Polish immigrants who settled in West and Center Rutland came from Galacia, near Cracow. Shortly after they arrived, they established a church in West Rutland under the leadership of Father Valentine Mihulka.[130]

Workers undertook the wide range of tasks required to quarry, finish, move and sell marble. The production of marble was no simple task. The production of marble involved several distinct elements: 1) the quarry, 2) transportation, 3) the mill yard, 4) the finishing mill and 5) the office work.

The range of jobs, according to the 1880 Non-Agricultural Census, began outdoors with the quarryman, sawyer, cutter, teamster and derrick operator and their support services, such as the blacksmith and the stable hand. Inside the mills were workers such as the polisher, the turner and the machinist who shaped the marble, as well as the highly skilled sculptor-artisan who created

In the years before automation, both oxen and horses hauled large blocks of marble into place. *Courtesy of Rutland Historical Society.*

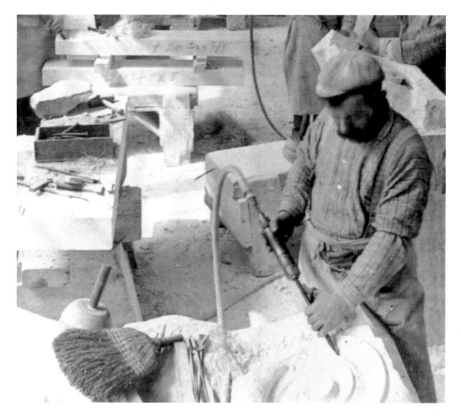

This marble carver uses a carving tool powered by air compressed by the electricity generated by the waterfall. *Courtesy of Vermont Marble Museum.*

the artwork. The grader then evaluated the marble. A marble saw maker, like thirty-six-year-old Edward Ryan in 1880, was responsible for checking and making the blades for the sawyers. The boxer, aided by the dockworker, readied the marble for shipping. The shipping clerk, the office worker and the bookkeeper did the billing and created the paper trail. Beyond the mill was the sales force. Traveling agents such as Edwin Sayre, forty-two and born in New York, helped arrange contracts. Distribution centers were established throughout the country with local managers and agents.[131]

The work began at the quarry, and for the quarrymen in particular, the workday was long. It began in the morning from spring into fall, as soon as there was enough sunlight. In West Rutland, the angelus bell from St. Bridget's Irish Roman Catholic Church, at the top of the hill on Pleasant Street overlooking the quarries, rang to signal the beginning of the workday about six o'clock in the morning. The long day added to the danger. In 1886, one of the demands of the Workingmen's caucus was to reduce the workday to a ten-hour day.[132] In November, when the daylight hours became shorter and the weather turned colder, the marble companies usually reduced the hours for the workers, and by December the quarries and mills shut down for an indefinite time period. Up to the 1880s, the quarrymen were laid off on December 1 of each year and usually not rehired until April 1.[133]

Besides the long workday, another issue that all workers faced—especially immigrants who had no family to fall back on—was when they would be paid. The pattern throughout the nineteenth century was for workers to be paid on a monthly basis, and that meant at times there would be a cash flow crisis. A local lawyer from Fair Haven wrote to the *Herald* on August 27, 1886:

> *The practice of monthly payment of wages especially in our larger industries is of long standing. A less excusable habit has generally obtained of delaying payments to the 15th or 20th of the succeeding month. So it is about six weeks from the time the poor laborer commences work before he receives a dollar of his earnings, and then, only about two-thirds of a month's earnings he has actually earned. As but few common laborers are blessed with the sufficient capital to meet the current expenses of a month or six weeks, the only alternative is the deplorable one of running into debt.*[134]

Although an effective quarry worker (typically Irish in the 1850s) in the course of a day could cut as much as five square feet of the rock face, the average was a block three square feet by as many feet deep as the channel ran. The *Geology of Vermont* in 1861 describes the salary and job of a quarryman—the most dangerous and arduous work of all jobs in the marble industry—in these terms:

> *It costs twenty-eight cents a foot to get channels cut. A good workman could cut from five to ten feet—that is to say, a groove one foot deep and from five to ten feet in length—per diem, which yielded a daily income to the workman of $1.40 to $2.80. A quarryman worked 10–12 hours, six days a week, working with a drill-chisel, boring into hard marble.*[135]

From early morning to evening, the men stood in the open quarry, which workers simply referred to as the "hole," exposed to brutal sun in the summer and soaking rain in the spring and the fall, using ball drills to drill channels and cut chunks of the stone. The summer heat could be ferocious, and the glare from the white marble could pierce the eyes. Cotton sheets thrown over immense wooden racks shaded the cuts of marble, enabling the drillers to see what they were doing and protecting their eyes somewhat from the glare.

Workers relied on hand tools or explosives in the first half of the nineteenth century. The worker's hand tools consisted of the drill, the hammer and the wedge. Using the drill and the hand hammer, the worker made a row of holes a few inches apart along the layer or stratum, perpendicular to the plane of stratification. He then filled in each hole of the row with three wedges, shaped so that the worker could drive each wedge into the other and widen the hole, a process called "plugs and feathers." As the worker continued to strike each plug with a sharp blow of his hammer, he gradually separated the marble from its bed. The combined splitting force of the plugs and feathers eventually became great enough to separate the rock.

A second method was the use of explosives. Explosives loosened large blocks of marble but would often damage the fragile marble. Quarrymen in the late nineteenth century also used a heavy steel ball weighing several tons to break up large blocks of marble. Quarry workers could use yet another method, which combined a power saw, an abrasive such as sand and water as a lubricant and coolant. The worker used the saw to make a cut or narrow channel and then expanded the cut by a wedge or blasted it. He deepened the channel until wedges could be inserted, freeing the sides of the large marble blocks. Next the sawyers removed the key block at the end of each course, which allowed other workmen known as gadders to bore holes eight inches apart into the bottom of the block.[136]

Division of labor separated the gadders from the sawyers; gadders, like their predecessors, forced wedges, now called gadding pins, into the holes (plugs and feathers). Once a large block of marble had been detached, the worker could use the plug-and-feather method to cut the stone into smaller sections. This part of the process demanded great skill to make sure that the vulnerable marble was not damaged. The channeling and wedging process worked well for quarrying marble and other soft stones such as sandstone and limestone but was not suitable for granite, a harder stone.[137]

Later in the nineteenth century, workers used steam-driven channeling machines, or channelers. The channeling machines made two parallel cuts (or grooves) called channels in the marble about five feet apart. Once the channel machine had gouged its way into the marble surface, equally deep channels at either end of a "course" enabled the piece to be removed as a square block. The self-propelled machines moved a cutting edge back and forth along the line on the rock bed that the worker had selected.

Once the marble had been quarried, the next step was to get it to the mill for processing. First, sleds pulled by horses or oxen carried marble slabs to the top of the quarry slope. Where the route was particularly strenuous or dangerous, oxen were preferred over horses, because oxen seemed to have more steady control.

With the advent of the railroad and the crane, operators could load the large blocks onto and off from railroad cars. At first the cranes were steam-powered, but later, about the beginning of the twentieth century, electric-powered cranes were used. In 1905 and 1906, the work site at Proctor began to use electricity, the other sites followed shortly thereafter. Machinery more sophisticated and powerful allowed workers to move heavier blocks of marble more quickly. The Vermont Marble Company, an innovator in its own right, began to generate electric power at Proctor in 1905 and 1906 and used it inside and outside of the plant with its machinery to off-load the marble from the sleds and to process the marble.

Once inside the mill, the third major step was cutting the marble blocks into smaller sizes by using gang saws. The fourth step involved finishing and carving the product. Finishing consisted of placing the slab on a rubbing bed—a large, horizontal, revolving iron disc. Sand and water trickled onto the disc, acting as abrasives to scrub away rough protrusions from the marble surface, producing a dull but smooth surface on the marble. The marble could then be placed on a lathe to form columns or urns that were then cut and polished. Polishing was accomplished through the use of a machine-driven rotating buffer.

The carvers were considered artists and had the highest status. They were one of the highest-paid groups within the building trades.[138] Carvers used three basic types of chisels. Points are used first for roughing out the design into the stone; then toothed chisels are used to smooth the faceting left by the points and to determine the compound curves. Tooth chisels (also claw tools), finally, shape and model the forms. Smaller and smaller chisels inscribe finer and finer details.

Marble takes one final step. After sanding and applying rouge (if used), a worker sealed the surface with oxalic acid or tin oxide to protect it and preserve the shine. The worker had to be very careful, especially with the highly corrosive acid, which would attack any organic matter such as skin or eyes. The acid literally melted the surface marble crystals together, and the worker then rinsed any remaining oxalic acid away with water. Although oxalic acid was more hazardous to the worker to apply, it was often the manufacturer's choice because it produced better results more easily and with less polishing than the tin oxide. Finally, the finishers let the surface dry completely before applying a topical wax. Now it was ready to be boxed, shipped, distributed to distant points and sold.

Management at various levels tried to ensure that the process worked smoothly. Assistant foremen and foremen controlled production; directly above them were assistant supervisors and supervisors. Supportive to the worker and the company was the company store. Management needed its own support staff of clerks and office workers. Workers often came from worlds apart. Ebenezer Tremayer, born in England, was the manager of the company store; Edward Kouchborn, born in Canada, clerked in the store at Sutherland Falls. Above everyone else was, as the 1880 Census phrased it, the "producer and owner," Redfield Proctor. With his political and economic connections, Redfield Proctor would use his power and influence from the 1870s to the 1900s at the state and national level to protect and advance the marble interests.[139]

To help make workers more conscious of safety at work, the Vermont Marble Company published a handbook of rules in the workers' native languages. The forty-six rules covered all hazardous aspects of the marble production. The first rule emphasized an awareness that all workers should maintain. "The time to be careful is before the accident occurs," the rule book stated. It emphasized not "doing anything to detract from the order and the efficiency of the plant" or distracting others from their work. Then the rules moved to concern for the new worker. More seasoned workers were encouraged to look out for new employees and make them aware of safety in the mill.

Since there was a danger of fire or combustion with dust in the air, workers were not allowed to smoke during work hours, and in some sections of the plant no smoking was allowed at any time. Smoking also might detract from the worker's concentration. Since the mill contained high-speed machinery for cutting and polishing, loose clothing could catch in the machinery, so it was not allowed. Workers were told to wear their jackets inside their coveralls. Moving the slabs also presented a danger. Since slabs of marble were dangerous, workers had a set of rules about them, such as "Don't get in front of slabs that are standing on edge unless they are properly braced." Eye injuries were another concern, so workers were told to "always wear goggles." Quarry workers had four rules in particular:

> *When working in the quarry, don't get in front of the blocks or follow too closely behind the block that is being drawn out of the layer. The rope or chain may break and hit you.*
>
> *Don't go near a blast unless you are sure that all of the holes have gone off.*
>
> *Don't ride out of the quarry on derrick hooks or on loads that are being hoisted, or ride on loads under cranes.*
>
> *In handling rock in the quarry, look out that you don't catch your fingers or toes under it.*[140]

Of all the marble workers, the quarry workers faced the most hazardous conditions. John B. Brewster was finishing up work on the evening of July 28, 1855, at the Rutland Marble Company's Quarry Number Two in West Rutland; suddenly, an overhanging block of rock two hundred feet long gave way. The huge boulder was hurled down, raining twenty feet of rock onto the pump that removed water from the quarry. It narrowly missed Brewster, who had checked the pump only minutes before and then had left the quarry. The damage to the quarry and the pump was $10,000 and delayed a reopening of the quarry until winter.[141]

As this example shows, the top of the quarry could often be dangerous for people below. In August 1867, a group of men at the Rutland Marble Company were moving wood to be used for fuel for one of the steam stonecutters. One of the wood-carrying men stumbled; his burden tumbled into the quarry, striking August Porterman on the head with such force that it fractured his skull and fatally injured him. The falling wood also struck Carl Rodmeracker, causing severe injuries, but doctors believed that he would be able to recover.[142]

Anyone who entered the quarry or worked around it had to be careful. Inattention could be deadly. William F. Barnes, the owner of the successful Barnes quarries, was involved in a fatal accident when a large block of marble fell on him in a quarry on Friday, May 5, 1871. He was given little chance of recovery but lingered on. On Saturday, he seemed to rally in the afternoon, but the next day he lost ground; about nine o'clock in the evening he died.[143]

The Vermont Marble Company attempted to keep workers on its payroll after accidents by finding a more suitable job for them. The paternalism of the company engendered worker loyalty when the first- and second-generation Proctors ran the company. Carrus Belmord, for instance, was a marble worker whose eyes were damaged in an explosion at the quarry in 1890. The company shifted him to "taking sand from the ditches that run the mill."[144]

The worst of all accidents, known as the "Quarry Horror," occurred on February 10, 1893. In the West Rutland Quarry Number Three, at a depth of 250 feet, a 65-foot marble block—about eighteen inches in width and with a thickness of two or three inches—came loose, killing five men and injuring ten others.[145] The workers who were killed came from each of the major immigrant ethnic groups: Alex Blumberg (Swede), Edward Powers (Irish), Felix Bellaire (French) and William Lukas and Frank Kulig (both Polish). The local paper reported that the survivors suffered from a "badly jammed neck" and "bruised shoulders."[146]

In the summer of 1893, tragedy continued. Anton Bakarsok, a Pole, was instantly killed and Frank Kappa and Frank Bick were badly injured in an accident at the new Vermont Marble Company quarry in West Rutland when a block of marble that had been lifted from the quarry fell back in. It had been sitting at the quarry edge, waiting to be transferred. Workers attempted to hoist it farther, but after it had been hoisted a few feet, the derrick chain broke, and the twelve-ton block fell. Rolling off the landing, it fell one hundred feet and struck the projecting side of the quarry, breaking into a thousand pieces. These pieces were hurled into the quarry twenty feet below.

The foreman reported to the paper:

> *Bakarsok, Kappa and Bick* [three quarrymen] *had evidently heard the noise of the falling block and were standing about 50 feet away from the point directly under the block…A piece of the block, that I should think weighed about 250 pounds, struck Bakarsok in the back and knocked him against a marble pier. I think the fall crushed his head. The other men were struck by pieces of the broken block.*[147]

Using drills in the quarry could also be dangerous. Wayne Sarcka recalls how his father lost one eye and injured the other, becoming nearly blind, operating a drill on the quarry floor in Florence. The Vermont Marble Company transferred him to the mills in Proctor, "where vision was less important."[148]

In the fall of 1893, Nils Olson, a forty-six-year-old Swedish foreman, died after being accidentally hit in the stomach by the head of a sledgehammer when it broke off. Another workman had been using it. Peritonitis developed rapidly despite the immediate medical attention he received. Olson was struck on Tuesday and died from the complications on Thursday. The Vermont Marble Company paid the $500 death benefit to his heirs.

Machinery within the mill was dangerous, as well. At the Columbian Mills, a marble block fell off a rubbing bed, badly scraping and bruising Dan Callahan's leg. The day before, "Timothy Murphy, working at the same bed, lost the great toe from his right foot and had the other foot jammed by a similar accident."[149] John Dary, a Swede who had spent the majority of his years in Proctor, was instantly killed in 1892 when he was caught in a pulley that was turning at a speed of ninety revolutions per minute at the Proctor Mill. He had started to go overhead to "screw up" a gang when his lamp went out, leaving him in total darkness. His clothing caught between a belt and a rapidly revolving pulley, drawing him into the turning gear works.[150]

Joseph Nason, a Pole, had both bones of his leg broken above the ankle at the Vermont Marble Company. He was lifting a marble slab with a bar when the bar slipped, letting the slab fall across his leg. On February 15, 1893, Robert Tracey, who worked in the mill of the Vermont Marble Company, was seriously injured about 11:30 a.m. when a marble block tipped over, breaking and crushing both of his legs. Tracey, age thirty-six, died in the hospital that evening. He left a wife, three children and a brother.[151]

The mill yard, where marble was loaded on train cars, was yet another dangerous place. A seventeen-year-old marble worker named Assellin was run over by a loaded train in West Rutland about 5:30 p.m. on July 24, 1888, cutting off his right leg and severely crushing his left leg. The local doctor, Dr. Hanrahan, amputated the crushed leg at 3:00 a.m. in an attempt to save the young man, but Assellin lingered for just a few more hours before he died.[152]

In February 1906, William M. Snyder, twenty-seven, of Forest Street in Rutland City, had been sent to Proctor to get a derailed freight car back on the track near the marble finishing shop. The car slipped off the jacks that were lifting it back toward the track; Snyder was squeezed between the heavily loaded freight car and the marble wall of the loading deck, near the marble finishing shop. He was compressed into a space of less than six inches, and his life was "crushed out instantly." Dr. Hack, the railroad physician, examined the body, but nothing could be done.[153]

Accidents came from a person falling as well as objects falling on the person. In 1902, Frank Skodowski, "a Polander" about twenty years old, suffocated in a pile of sand. He had climbed on top of a pile of sand used in the marble-smoothing process. Skodowski apparently slipped into the sand discharge chute and was followed by a pile of sand, which filled in around him and cut off all attempts to save him.[154] In the mill yard, Lawrence Romano, "a Polander," fell from the old coal shed trestle while unloading waste marble on June 6, 1904. He died the following afternoon as a result of an abscess on the brain. He was twenty-eight years old and, according to the local newspaper, had no relatives in this country.[155]

In February 1906, one man was killed and two were seriously injured when a locomotive rolled into the Vermont Marble Company machine shop. The collision occurred at 5:50 p.m., toward the end of the workday. The cars, one loaded with marble blocks and the other with marble bases for rock face underpinning, had been left shortly after 5:00 p.m. on the middle track of the engine house. The grade had a steep incline, extending to the machine shop in an easterly direction, a distance of about 1,300 feet. The cars started rolling back about 5:45 p.m., gaining momentum rapidly, and crashed into the locomotive just as it was about to enter the shop. Andrew Kokman, the engineer, was caught in the wreckage and was so badly scalded by escaping steam that he died the following day in the hospital. The fireman escaped injury by jumping from the train. In the same incident, a railway car collided with another flatcar, injuring a young Polish immigrant quarryman, Alexander Bardjewics, nineteen. He had been working in the mill yard when the runaway railroad car struck him, breaking both his legs so badly that he was listed in critical condition.[156]

Just three days later, Joseph Backarrack, twenty-five, was electrocuted, along with another worker named Janizewski, thirty-two. Later that year, Ignace Siwek, nineteen, was "crushed by a car in the quarry." He suffered a compound fractured skull, and both legs were fractured, along with his ribs. He died an hour after the accident. A year later, on November 30, Joseph Ruoka, twenty-six, was "killed instantly by being caught in shafting." And about a week later, on December 5, Karol Swientski, twenty-two, was in an accident that "fractured ribs-thigh and arms"; he lived for six hours after the accident.[157]

Local immigrant societies and churches provided some emotional and financial support. The larger the immigrant group—such as the Irish, the French and Italians—the more likely the social and institutional structures would provide aid. The sense of identity of work and place was essential. They were marble workers, and ethnic and religious ties functioned as important sub-communities. Marble workers attended ethnic churches that reinforced the sense of solidarity. Their homes were clustered near the work site, often in view of the church.

At the end of their long and dangerous workday of twelve hours in the long summer days in the 1850s and 1860s, the worker looked forward to returning to his home. The home was a place located within walking distance of work and was most often rented to the worker's family. Here the worker's family could plant a garden to supplement the family income. But there were dangers with family housing, as well.

CHAPTER 5

AT HOME

Housing and Health

Before the formation of the Vermont Marble Company, most workers in the marble industry of the 1850s and 1860s worked for small companies and lived in company houses of every size and shape. The most common characteristic of the early dwellings was poor construction, and they were often tenements, housing ten large Irish families at a time. The worker, like his housing, was an extension of the company. Frequently, single workers lived in a boardinghouse, and many families lived in company-owned housing.[158]

Although some workers lived in Rutland, the three principal areas for marble worker housing were located in West Rutland, Center Rutland and Sutherland Falls. In West Rutland, the tenements were near the railroad tracks and the company store, which was on the east side of the swamp. In Sutherland Falls, the houses were near the mill or the cemetery; in Rutland, most of the houses were near St. Peter's Church, while in Center Rutland they were along West Street and Barrett's Hill. Some boardinghouses or tenement houses were suitable for families[159] and had six or seven rooms.

In November 1883, a tourist published a narrative of his vacation to the Green Mountain State and commented on the workers and the housing:

> *The common laborers are nearly all foreigners—French Canadians, Irish, Swedes—but they are temperate and orderly; strikes are rare; and here [Sutherland Falls], as in the other marble districts, the proprietors have shown themselves the friends of their employés by building neat little cottages, founding libraries and reading rooms, and endowing churches.*[160]

Boardinghouses like this served as homes for bachelors and married men whose families had not yet joined them. Boarders often received breakfast, a tin-pail midday meal and supper at these residences. *Courtesy of Rutland Historical Society.*

Vermont Marble Company built both duplexes like this one and single-family houses for its workers. They were then encouraged to buy their own homes from the company via automatic withdrawals from their paychecks. *Mike Austin Collection.*

At Home

Vermont Marble Company sold this house, on Barrett Hill in Rutland, to the Johnson family for ten dollars. *Johnson Family Collection.*

The West Rutland Company Store was built from marble blocks from the nearby quarries. These company stores provided credit and a variety of goods. *Courtesy of Rutland Historical Society.*

Vermont Marble Company donated the marble to build St. Bridget's Church in West Rutland. VMC employees donated their time, working at the end of shifts and on Sundays. *Courtesy of Rutland Historical Society.*

Christ the King Church, at the top of Gouger Hill in Rutland, was also built from donated marble. Ethnic churches were located in Rutland and throughout the region. Christ the King was viewed as a "lace curtain Irish" church, situated on a hill. *Mike Austin Collection.*

St. Domenic's Catholic Church in Proctor is another example of a church constructed from the marble of the region and built by the workers. In style it is very similar to the Christ the King Church in Rutland. *Mike Austin Collection.*

The Vermont Marble Company, unlike its earlier predecessors, worked more closely with the laborers to provide housing, often building and then selling houses to them. The houses would stay in the Vermont Marble Company title until the workers had paid a large enough equity that a financial institution felt comfortable in picking up a loan for the remainder. It could be argued that the company was patronizing to the workers, but if so, the workers also sought this patronage.

At this time, little negative connotation was attached to the word "tenement." The later tenements were duplex cottages, rented by workers and their families, which were clustered together in neighborhoods throughout the town. These houses were company houses, most frequently built on a common pattern. Many immigrant workers might have seen this type of congregate-housing as a step up from what they had left behind in Europe. They may have been tenants in Ireland or other places, but the political and social structure here was not as oppressive as it was back home. The marble workers were not rich, but they had a chance to work their way out of the quarries into retail ventures or acquire inexpensive land for farming.

Most of the families would grow small gardens to save money and provide an additional source of food. Workers' family gardens were planted with potatoes, cabbages and other vegetables, raising a large part of their winter food supply. The garden provided them with food when the quarry had shut down or had limited hours during the winter months. The storing of food and preparing for winter was essential. If they did not prepare for winter, they possibly would go hungry unless their neighbors or the church aided them.[161]

Nearly every company furnished its workers with a "company store." Unfortunately, such stores frequently gouged the workers who shopped there. Although there were also independent stores in the community, marble workers most often shopped at the company store; it charged higher prices than its competitors did, but workers could charge their purchases. The workers complained that they seldom received any actual wages; instead, they received credit to shop only at the company store, where prices were usually 33 percent higher than at other merchants.[162]

Many families had a cow, a few pigs and chickens. With the milk from the cow, the family could make its own butter, but other necessary goods—such as a barrel of flour, sugar, coffee, tea and molasses—would have to come from the store. Raising household gardens and tending the cow and other livestock were part of wifely responsibilities and provided a sense of pride

Men and livestock combined their efforts to move marble outside the Vermont Marble Company in Proctor. The overhead hoist provided much of the lifting power to move large blocks. *Courtesy of Vermont Marble Museum.*

and also an economic contribution; the husband was away at the quarry or mill from early in the morning until late in the afternoon.

Another issue that confronted the worker and housing was sanitation. At first, it was not a major problem. Because of the value and scarcity of the food, one worker recalls, "There was very little garbage to dispose of in my early days. The first I recall was simply thrown out in back. Later, the village [Proctor] serviced weekly a box at every street. Garbage was collected in a horse drawn dump cart and in our area was carted a short distance away and dumped in the pine wood."[163]

In the back was the garden; workers recycled the leftover food into a compost heap or buried it directly to nourish the soil.

Management houses were, not surprisingly, more expansive and elaborate. In nearly all cases, however, and Redfield Proctor was no exception, owners and management lived relatively close to the quarries or mills.

Unlike the company-controlled housing in West Rutland and Proctor, the worker houses in Rutland were generally individually owned. Most marble workers lived near St. Peter's, a Roman Catholic church located in the poorer section of town near the railroad tracks. Meadow and Forest Streets, parallel to each other, represented the heart of this district, which was distinct from other marble worker neighborhoods because non-marble workers lived there as well. Worker houses were also located in Center Rutland near the falls, along what is now Route 4. Barrett Hill, a section of Center Rutland adjacent to the falls, contained many marble worker homes dating back to the marble mills, when the Irish were the primary immigrants working in the marble industry.

Because of the influx of immigrants, marble companies built cheap, easily constructed housing based on a uniform pattern. Companies did not want to waste valuable land, so worker housing in West Rutland, Rutland, Center Rutland and Sutherland Falls was built on rectangular plots close together.

Many of the worker houses, including those in the town that would be renamed Proctor, were very close to the road and faced the street. There was no front yard for most of the houses and, at best, little yardage for others. At the rear, usually at the corner of the lot, was the outhouse. The small duplex cottage shared one roof, with one family or group living in either side. Living close together, neighbors were very much aware of one another and could share with one another.

Unlike the slums in the major cities at that time, or even compared to the high rises of the twentieth century, the population density was relatively low. The housing itself never went beyond two floors. The closeness of the houses had advantages and disadvantages. Since the houses were close together, each house provided a buffer to the wind and snow in the winter months rather than being exposed in an open terrain. But at the same time, this closeness created a threat from fires, which could spread quickly from one house to another.

Each family had a separate entrance. The house was divided in half, with an upstairs and a downstairs for each family, and each unit had its own chimney. On the rear of the house was a lean-to shed for storage. In front of the shed and in the middle of the house was the kitchen; it served not only for preparing meals but also, because it was in the center and on the lower floor, as a source of warmth. Off the kitchen were a small pantry and a room that could also be used as a bedroom. Frequently known as the "birthing room," this central sleeping space was warmer than the rest of the house during the winter because it backed up against the kitchen chimney. It was a place for babies to be born, infants or toddlers to nap or for arthritic seniors to warm their bones; it was somewhat undisturbed by household activity.

Often the houses were constructed in low areas at the bottom of the hill, as they were in Proctor, or near the swamp, as they were in West Rutland. Soot and pollution settled in the lowest part of the land. In addition to industrial pollution, there was air pollution from the railroads that were close to the housing and work sites. Redfield Proctor's house, although near the mill, was at the top of the hill near Otter Creek and above the falls. Thus, while somewhat exposed to the pollution, he and his family were not as exposed as many of the other workers.

A further danger was air pollution from the wood stoves. Wood was the primary source of fuel, both for heat and for cooking, and was stored behind the house. Burning wood contributed to the air pollution in the valley, adding its set of airborne dirt and chemicals to the industrial pollution from the mill and the railroads. As late as the 1990s, some residents recalled the smog that covered the valley when they were growing up in the 1950s before the railroad engines switched from steam to diesel locomotives.[164] The *Rutland Herald* in 1881 interpreted the pollution in a much more positive light:

> *Those who have been discomfited by the smoke with which the air has been filled the past few days will be glad to know that it is really beneficial, for, according to an exchange, "the more one breathes of it the better up to a reasonable point." The creosote, which has been taken into the lungs and through them carried into the blood since the murky season set in, is as good as a course of treatment by a physician. People who had toothache a week ago ought to be over their trouble by this time. Creosote, as its name implies, is a preserver of flesh. It is by virtue of this property that smoke preserves hams and other meats subjected to its influence. Creosote forms the base of a large part of the medicine which people take when the doctor prescribes it for them. It is good for hemorrhage, diarrhea, cholera morbus, cholera infantum, nausea, vomiting, toothache and a variety of other ailments. No one can say that the visitation of smoke at this time is not intended as an antidote for some disease that would be disastrous. It may save many people from cholera morbus brought on by overeating of watermelons and half-ripened fruits.[165]*

Pollution from the mills, locomotives and homes was certainly unsafe, but there were other dangers as well. The sparks from a locomotive could ignite a nearby house, or an improperly cleaned chimney could give rise to a fire.

Redfield Proctor faced many of the same problems of pollution and danger from fires as his managers and workers did. In 1882, the house owned by the Vermont Marble Company and occupied by then governor Proctor, caught fire about 10:30 p.m. on a Friday. Although arson was suspected at first, the fire was later classified as an accident. Redfield Proctor and his family were not at home at the time. The family had spent most of the winter in Boston, and a fire had been started in the furnace to warm the house for the Proctors, who were expected to return at the beginning of the week. The house was insured for $1,000 (1882), which was considered about half its value.[166]

Because the Vermont Marble Company had equipment, it was often involved in extinguishing fires in the town. For example, on January 6, 1909, the fire department of the Vermont Marble Company was called to put out what was later ascertained to be a fire deliberately set. A Polish immigrant and his wife were both arrested; only he was jailed because the couple had small children who "needed her care." The *Herald* made an interesting observation: "This class of foreigners think [*sic*] as long as they pay their insurance policy premiums they have a right to set the property on fire."[167]

Accidents threatened commercial property, as well. In the summer of 1894 at 1:30 p.m., a fire broke out in the finishing shop and threatened to spread to the Patterson and Haley Mills in Proctor, which were under one roof. Men rushed to the roof with buckets of water; others used marble as a barricade against the tin partitioned doors to prevent the spread of the fire.[168]

Besides the work-related accidents and sanitation that affected families, infectious diseases such as influenza, smallpox, diphtheria, typhus, scarlet fever or cholera could overwhelm a family and spread through these condensed neighborhoods. The year following the great Quarry Horror of 1893 was an especially troubling year to all of the families in the valley. Even before the Quarry Horror of February 10, 1893—which was the single largest accident for the Vermont Marble Company—and the outbreak of widespread infantile paralysis in the summer of 1894, the community of Rutland and the Vermont Marble Company took a proactive stance about healthcare.

The economic and population centers of the Marble Valley were located around Rutland. Rutland's nearest hospital was located at Castleton Medical

College (1818–61, later absorbed into Castleton State College), approximately twelve miles away. Because of the traveling distance to Castleton, many people injured and ill suffered at home and often in unsanitary conditions. A medical provider was needed in the Rutland area, where there would be more access to the growing population.

The first meeting to plan the hospital took place on May 8, 1891. Reverend Charles Niles of Trinity Episcopal Church hosted the meeting at his house, and Reverend George W. Phillips of the Congregational church was co-sponsor. By 1891, the Catholic population was a significant part of the community, so Reverend T.J. Gaffney of St. Peter's Catholic Church was invited, as was the Catholic priest from the French church.

In the fall of 1891, Redfield Proctor, aware of the need for a hospital, asked his son, Fletcher D. Proctor, then president of the Vermont Marble Company, to offer the committee the "Ripley House," west of the entrance to Evergreen Cemetery in Center Rutland, for a hospital building. The Proctors were also concerned that the hospital would be able to meet its ongoing expenses and so stipulated that the building would be rent-free for five years if the committee in return could raise $5,000 per year for the hospital's operation. Redfield Proctor would pledge a quarter of that amount, but the committee could only raise $488 and decided to refuse the offer.[169]

In March 1892, the committee received a gift of land from Julia and Evelyn Pierpoint. On May 3, 1893, they officially deeded four acres of land on Spring Street, now called State Street, to the committee for one dollar. The property was located near a new street that would be developed, later called Pierpoint Avenue. The Rutland Hospital would later be built on a street just above the Roman Catholic church, Immaculate Heart of Mary, a French nationalist church built, like many of the Catholic churches in the area, by quarry workers in their off hours.

The movement for better healthcare and access to that healthcare was a concern for Fletcher Proctor, son of Redfield and his successor as president of Vermont Marble. Fletcher Proctor saw healthcare as a corporate responsibility to his workers. Workers and the community would benefit and also identify with the company. Fletcher Proctor was instrumental in establishing the first industrial nursing program in the United States. The industrial nurse served the areas in which the marble company had sites. She pedaled her bicycle to make her rounds, dealing with the different immigrant languages. Medical services were primarily for the marble workers and their families and secondarily for other citizens of the town in which the marble company had locations. For the most part, this approach meant that the Proctors served the outlying areas rather than the downtown section of Rutland.

In 1895, Fletcher Proctor held several meetings to discuss the feasibility of hiring a district nurse. There were no public nurses at the time of Fletcher Proctor's plan, and he was embarking on an innovative community approach. The closest, both in concept and in implementation, seemed to be at the Waltham (Massachusetts) School of Nursing, where students of the Waltham School were sent out to individuals' homes with a graduate nurse

Ada Mayo Stewart became Vermont Marble Company's—and the nation's—very first industrial nurse in about 1895. *Courtesy of Rutland Historical Society.*

Vermont Marble Company created a local hospital at which workers and their families received free treatment. They treated workers who initially came from twenty-three different countries. *Courtesy of Rutland Historical Society.*

or a senior student present to instruct the students and to supervise the work. Students had to learn to do their best with the limited resources available. After searching, the Vermont Marble Company and the superintendent of nurses of the Waltham School selected Ada Mayo Stewart (1870–1945). She had special training in surgical and dispensary work and was already familiar with Vermont.

She traveled to the private homes by bicycle. Stewart delivered babies and attended to the physical ailments that afflicted the workers and their families. She later recalled that she ministered to the psychological needs of immigrant workers, as well. One woman who had been a dancer in one of Europe's royal theatres had come to America with her husband. The strain of drudgery and childbearing was too much for her; she became a drug addict and suffered a breakdown. One time, Stewart found her dressed in a gauze ballet costume, trying to perform the duties of a housewife.[170]

In 1895, given the success of the visiting nurse in Proctor, services were extended to both West Rutland and Center Rutland, where the Vermont Marble Company had other properties. The medical needs of the area served by the Vermont Marble Company, however, were greater than Stewart alone could handle, so more extensive plans were made for a hospital to be located in Proctor. The first hospital, located at 21 South Street in Proctor, was in reality a welfare project of the company and an extension of medical services provided to the company's workers. It was primarily intended for the company's employees and their families, but local residents of the communities in which the company had branches would be admitted as paying patients.

The hospital was clearly an extension of the Vermont Marble Company's concern for the productive health of its workers, but it was also good community relations. To involve the community more in the project, so that the hospital was not viewed as completely run by the company, the management of the hospital was transferred to a representative board of local people who had places on all committees.

The board of management of the Proctor Hospital consisted of people of the community, from business, professions and the home. Fourteen of the sixteen members of the first board were either employed by Vermont Marble or married to an employee. The president of the board was George Davis, a foreman. Other members included Fletcher Proctor himself, a vice-president, two other foremen, a clerk and two stenographers—one of them Miss Carrie Lane. In addition to Miss Lane, five other women served on the board: Mrs. Redfield Proctor, two wives of cutters, the daughter of a foreman and Mrs. H.J. Banker, wife of a Methodist minister. Aside from Mrs. Banker, the other nonemployee on the board was Dr. H.H. Swift, an attending physician.[171]

The Vermont Marble Company continued its moral and financial support of the hospital and other community ventures. The connection with the Waltham School of Nursing continued, so that the first graduate nurses (Alice Kirsting and Sarah A. Barclay), the first four matrons of the Proctor Hospital and the first two district nurses were all from the Waltham School. Ada Stewart was the matron, with Katherine Field and Harriet Stewart serving as nurses and Mae Landers and Minnie Negus as student nurses.

On the very day the Proctor Hospital opened, it was nearly filled. The illnesses of the earliest patients indicate the seriousness of the diseases that affected the workers and the immigrants. The hospital had five typhoid cases, and two of those patients could speak no English, thus making the delivery of services even more complicated. One of the typhoid patients was so ill that he was delirious.

The hospital was in service until 1904, when a new hospital on Ormsbee Avenue replaced it. This second hospital was also subsidized by the Vermont Marble Company and was in use from 1904 to 1973. With the rise of population after World War II, the hospital shifted its mission to specializing in maternal care, but it still maintained many of its other concerns.

In 1894, a medical tragedy struck the valley. Infantile paralysis, or poliomyelitis, spread through the valley and struck young children. Families felt powerless and did not know what to do. The first known epidemic in the United States occurred in the summer of 1894 in the valley. Dr. Charles S. Caverly, president of the Vermont Board of Health, reported the incident in the *Yale Medical Journal* in November 1894.[172] From June 17 to September 1, Caverly noted the disease raging through central Vermont, affecting 123 children directly. All but 6 of these cases occurred in the valley. In 1910, 1911, 1912 and 1913, the disease flared up again throughout the state.

Caverly also noted that the "so-called laboring classes were oftenest affected,"[173] but not out of proportion to their numbers. He recorded that the general, sanitary conditions of pure air, food and water did not lead him to conclude the disease resulted from poor environmental conditions.

In the 1910 epidemic of polio, with the heightened sense of nativism that affected the country because of increased number of immigrants arriving in the last decade, Caverly was careful to note the nationalities that were affected by the outbreak in the state.

During the year 1914, the outbreak was the most severe, surpassing the outbreak of 1894. In response, the Proctor family set up a sanitarium, aided Caverly in his treatment and made an anonymous gift to the Vermont Department of Public Health. Treatment for the inflicted was largely massage, muscle exercise and the less regarded galvanic electricity. So alarming was the anxiety surrounding the outbreak in 1914 that Governor John Graham attended a health board meeting at which the following statement was approved restricting large gatherings. It read, in part:

> *In the past years we have had reason to think that large general gatherings of people from many towns have distributed this infection. August and*

September in past years have been our worst months as far as this disease is concerned. In view of these facts…[w]hen one or more cases develop in any town the local board of health should take action either prohibiting all public gatherings or excluding all children under 16 years of age from gatherings, also from lunch, soda water, ice cream counters and other public eating and drinking places. It is hereby ordered that no fairs, Chautauquas, street carnivals or circuses be held in the State of Vermont until further notice.

By order of the State Board of Health
Charles F. Dalton
(Secretary)[174]

Caverly advised that the precautions taken for scarlet fever and diphtheria should be applied to dealing with this present crisis. In the uncertainty of the 1910 epidemic, Caverly advised health officers in Vermont:

Let every physician learn from you that this disease is reportable. Enforce the laws as to reporting diseases that are "infectious and dangerous to the public health" as regards poliomyelitis. Enforce the "full quarantine" in this disease. Disinfect and clean up after the acute state is passed, as you would after diphtheria.[175]

Caverly examined the locations where the diseases struck. In the case of the 1894 epidemic, he noted that, at the southern end of Rutland where the East Creek and the Otter Creek joined, the water transported a large amount of sewage. In the summer months, when the water was low, the sewage-contaminated stream might contribute to the spread of the disease. He also examined the housing of the afflicted. Workers lived under the possibility that the epidemic could come again at any time and threaten their families. How you could protect yourself and your family was a medical, social and political issue. Workers wanted more control over their lives and began to organize.

CHAPTER 6

THE CHALLENGE OF
THE WORKERS

Like Pullman of Illinois or the Lowells in Massachusetts, Redfield Proctor was very much aware that political power and influence could benefit and protect his interests, whether in the community, the state or the nation. At the national level, he used his political influence both in and out of office to seek protective tariffs for marble. Applying the policies of corporate paternalism and welfare capitalism, he helped to shape Rutland, particularly those sections of Rutland where his company had a presence, making the town a model industrial community. Sober, hardworking, moral and thrifty, like many other influential industrialists, he saw the town in which he lived (or had his primary interest) as an extension of himself. Together, his political, economic and social worlds created a unified galaxy of power, a key factor in his support of the movement to partition the existing town of Rutland into four political units: Rutland, Rutland Town, West Rutland and Proctor. When Sutherland Falls became a separate town and received the name of Proctor, the new name was a public acknowledgement of the social and political influence of Redfield Proctor.

By the 1880s, distrust and tension had grown between the marble and agricultural interests in the outlying districts and commercial interests concentrated in the village. More local control, in the eyes of division proponents, meant a more fair and equitable distribution of resources. As early as the 1870s, sentiment for a division of the town from the village had been growing.[176]

A consensus was growing that greater local control would be in the best interest of all.[177] Nevertheless, the division did not occur until the power of

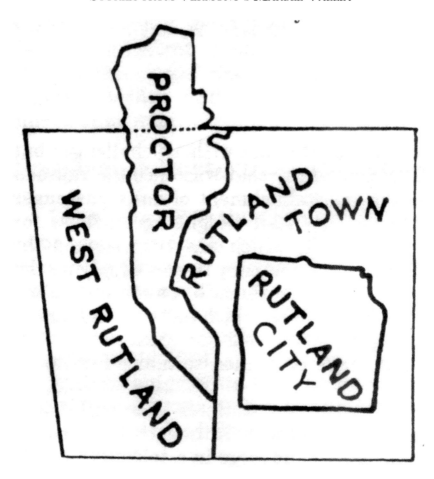

The original Rutland grant was encompassed within the rectangle. In the power struggle among the rural, city and marble interests, the area was divided among competing and self-protective interests. Rutland City became the "donut hole." *Courtesy of Rutland Historical Society.*

the local elites was challenged by local workers. In the mid-1880s, with the influx of immigrants, labor began to challenge the system more directly and confront the Republican Anglo-Saxon dominance of power. The challengers to the Republican Party were the Democratic Party, the Knights of Labor and the Labor Party. In response, the elites sought to consolidate power, redistricting the town into sections to divide and isolate immigrant power. Some workers saw an advantage in division because they could control their sections and see to it that tax money was not drawn off to support the privileged village.

From the viewpoints of workers and some of the rival elites, Rutland Village was the banking and railroad center, fostered by the old guard, such as the Clement family, who held sway in the city. Instead of being overwhelmed by sheer numbers of workers, Rutland could be divided into Rutland Village (the city), where both immigrants and the old guard lived; West Rutland, where many of the workers and immigrants lived; Rutland Town, a farming area; and Sutherland Falls, the center of the financial empire of the Vermont Marble Company and the residence of Redfield Proctor.

From the viewpoint of the existing elites with deep roots in Rutland, Redfield Proctor was a carpetbagger, trading on the personal connections he had established in the war. He wanted to thwart the Clement and Dorr faction by supporting the division of Rutland rather than advocating city status for the area. Proctor had come to Rutland because Rutland was a dynamic and growing center of commercial activity. After setting up a law partnership on Merchants Row in the heart of the new commercial Rutland, he entered the marble industry and played the major role in redeveloping it into the most lucrative segment of Vermont's economy. Proctor vaulted to the forefront economically, politically and socially, straining relations between the old rich and the new rich. The more successful the Proctors became, the more some in the old guard resented their sweeping power.

In 1881, Redfield Proctor was the wealthiest individual in Rutland Town (as yet undivided), with real and personal property valued at $278,000 and an interest in the Vermont Marble Company valued at $450,000. Other powerful families were the Clements, the Baxters and the Ripleys. Charles Clement, whose money originally had come from marble and banking, owned property valued at $257,000.[178] The Clement political and financial interest was tied to Rutland Village, which would become Rutland City. H.H. Baxter also had derived his wealth from marble, and his real and personal property was valued at $191,000. Baxter's primary interests, like those of the Clements, were centered on Rutland Village. The Ripleys, also old marble money, were now down the social and political list. Their area of interest was Center Rutland, which became part of Rutland Town. Socially, the Ripleys' interests focused on the village as well. All three of these powerful families were centering much of their attention on the growing financial sector.[179] William Ripley was president and Edward Ripley was vice-president of the Rutland County National Bank. Horace H. Baxter was president and Jonathan Baxter vice-president of the Baxter National Bank.

Charles, Percival and Wallace Clement were the owners of Clement and Sons, dealers in investment securities.[180]

The Clements were the chief political and social rivals to the Proctors. The Clement family had come to Rutland about 1842 as the marble industry was beginning its transformation. The family had predated the Proctors in the marble industry, but the Clements, while an old, established family in comparison to the Proctors, had not been as spectacularly successful. Charles Clement and a partner, named Porter, were in the retail business in Center Rutland as early as 1846. The Clement & Gilmore mill shows up on an 1854 map of Center Rutland.[181] In June 1855, the mill had sixteen saw gangs and produced 120,000 feet of marble per year. Clement & Gilmore originated

P.W. Clement came from a marble family and resented the upstart influence of Proctor in the marble business and politics. Clement contended with Redfield Proctor on many fronts, starting a rival bank and a newspaper that bashed the "Proctor machine" and Vermont Marble Company efforts whenever possible. *Courtesy of Rutland Historical Society.*

Redfield Proctor about the time of the division of Rutland. Proctor protected his marble interests and extended them into the original areas of Pittsford. *Courtesy of Rutland Historical Society.*

with a partnership, the firm of Barnes, Clement & Gilmore. Barnes was one of the earliest of the major marble entrepreneurs. The firm later became Clement & Gilmore, and about 1870 or 1872 it became Clement & Sons. The Clement National Bank was organized in 1883, located on the ground floor of the Clement Block. In the opinion of 1890 journalist J.P. McKinney, the board contained "the gentlemen representing the most wealthy and enterprising elements of the community."[182]

Percival W. Clement, born in 1846, was educated by private tutors at home and graduated in 1864 from St. Paul's School in Concord, New Hampshire. He then went on for further tutoring at Middlebury before he went to Trinity College in Hartford, Connecticut. What had propelled Clement into this comfortable life was the family marble fortune, but in the 1870s the Proctors began to supplant the Clement family's place in society and political and economic power. The *Rutland Herald* became a Clement mouthpiece. Albert Tuttle formed the Herald and Globe Association in 1873 and "enticed as early as 1882" Percival W. Clement to be editor. By 1886, Clement appeared "in firm control defeating on a policy matter the forces of the Proctor family."[183] Having gained control of the paper, Clement was now able to further his own political, social and economic ambition and, to a lesser degree, that of his allies.

The Clements cast themselves as leaders of a city-oriented vision with all its promise of the future. However, the Clement family interests, like those of the Proctor family, also extended far beyond Rutland Village. P.W. Clement became president of the Clement National Bank of Rutland and also president of the Rutland Railroad. The Clement holdings stretched into New York City, where he owned the Woodstock and Dunmore Hotels in New York City and Clement and Smith, a brokerage firm.[184]

Politically, the Clements and the Proctors were also rivals within the Republican Party in Vermont. The Proctors assumed a conservative position on moral issues such as religion and drinking. They were for the continued prohibition of alcohol in the state. Clement supported a local option law on alcohol. Although Vermont had been a dry state since the 1850s, the local option law would be a way that the city could bypass the general code. Thus certain districts would be exempt from the general community's traditions, which had been in place for half a century.

The workers were well aware of the concentrated power of the Clements and how the Clement interests seemed to favor the village of Rutland rather than the interests of the larger town. The workers felt that the village was already getting more than its fair share. From their viewpoint, the outlying districts were being sacrificed at the expense of the village. Redfield Proctor sided with the workers, especially his workers, who lived in these outlying districts, near the quarries and the headquarters of his company, and he used his political and economic interests to advance the division of Rutland.

Sutherland Falls (Proctor) and West Rutland were natural allies; their economic interests were based on marble, and both were outlying districts. Citizens of both areas felt that the village of Rutland was receiving proportionally more economic advantages at the expense of the other regions of the town. Social disturbances in the village, where rowdy young men might gather and harass citizens, troubled the sensitivity of Sutherland Falls and West Rutland, further alienating the outlying population. There was a certain perceived town-village difference of virtue. As early as 1867, commentators worried that the village showed a lower standard of morality in the new business district in the evening. The *Rutland Herald* commented:

The practice of a certain portion of our male inhabitants of lounging about street corners every evening for a couple of hours and indulging in the use of profane and obscene language, as such as passing ungentlemanly remarks upon every lady who happens to pass the points where they perch themselves is becoming unbearable and we hope some effort will be made to put a stop to it. The principal points where these person hold forth are the corners of Merchants' Row and West Streets, Merchants Row and Center streets and the intervening entrances, dry goods boxes and steps between these points, as well as upon the walk on Center Street leading from Merchants Row to Wales Street.[185]

In 1880, a group within the village petitioned the legislature to re-charter the village of Rutland as a city that would take in all three of the town's most heavily populated areas—Rutland Village, Sutherland Falls and West Rutland—and exclude only the most rural areas of the town. The advantage to the village would be a strong financial base to support the growth of the city. The traditional town meeting would be replaced by a body of men elected as ward representatives.

Rutland's 1880 population, as estimated by the *Rutland Herald*, was 12,150 and growing rapidly. By 1887, after West Rutland and Proctor had split off from Rutland Town, the population of the three towns was an estimated 16,000: 10,300 in Rutland, 4,000 in West Rutland and 1,700 in Proctor.[186]

To an extent, the differences in the sections of Rutland could be traced back to the 1700s, when the Congregational Church split into east and west parishes, each with its own meetinghouse. In 1773, the first Congregational Church and society was formed, but by 1787 divisions within the town had grown gradually. On January 25, 1787, eighty-five men from the east part of the town submitted a petition to the assembly for the division of the town into two religious societies. By the end of the year, the division into two societies had been granted.[187] Geographic distance in the town, not any theological differences, was the main reason for the division. Town meetings had alternated between the two meetinghouses, but on May 29, 1788, in a meeting held on the east side, in Rutland Village, the attendees voted to permanently suspend the meetings in the west.

Although many businesses closed for the day on town meeting day and the railroad gave free transportation so that any freeman could attend the event, the men who labored at the quarries, mills and farms of Rutland

Town resented having to go the greater distance to the east side each year. Disgruntled residents of the west side complained that infrastructure built with tax dollars, such as sidewalks and road improvement, took place only on the east side of the town.[188] By 1880, the argument was being cast in terms of democracy and virtue. The state had been "dry" since before the Civil War, but in the sinful village, men managed to find both the "potion" and women of ill repute.

The Dorrs of Dorr Road, another influential old guard family living near the village, also supported division. S.M. Dorr's argument was based on the traditional New England sense of democracy, but he believed that a division would have other advantages as well. Dorr, a financial investor, believed that the town had become too large in population for town meetings: "The true and simple democracy becomes impossible or at least impracticable." Dorr cited a request fifteen years earlier asking that voters be compelled "to have their names on a check-list, and that should confer upon an insignificant number or minority the right to demand a ballot by the check-list in the election of our town officers." The town, Dorr went on, had grown to the point that it needed a change; either "let the village of Rutland cut loose from the town and take a city charter for herself alone" or "organize the whole town under a city charter."[189]

Incorporating only the village of Rutland would leave the maintenance of bridges and support of the poor as a burden to the town while removing the wealthiest taxpayers.[190] The town of Rutland would not assume the debts currently owed by the village, as ensured by specific sections of the legislation. The only change in expense would be the addition of five polling places in place of the single large meeting. Dorr had a deceptive argument, but his position was consistent with village interests. His primary concern was to make the village a city. Either it would be city governed separately from the others or would be the most influential section of a larger city.[191] Seeing the vigorous opposition from the countryside around the village, the legislature turned down the request to give Rutland city status.[192]

The first practical signal of the upcoming partitioning of Rutland was noted in 1884 when Sutherland Falls, the corporate headquarters of the Vermont Marble Company, was incorporated as a village. Because the unincorporated village had not confined itself to the bounds of Rutland Town, the legislature approved the inclusion of a number of acres of land north along Otter Creek, taking them from the neighboring town of

Pittsford.[193] The area specified in the act encompassed sections from Rutland and Pittsford known as School District 21 in Pittsford, School District 14 in Rutland and the Piper farm, which bordered School District 14. These sections, in the wording of the act, "are hereby incorporated and made a body politic under the name of the village of Proctor…territory made be added to said village by vote of either the towns of Rutland or Pittsford."[194]

Seeing that greater local autonomy was bringing about more economic and social amenities, such as sidewalks and streetlighting, advocates of full autonomy for the marble areas supported a bill in the Vermont legislature in 1886 to set apart the towns of Proctor and West Rutland. This move was opposed by those who saw the village as a burgeoning center that needed the resources of the surrounding areas to achieve its potential. At the national level, a new labor organization, The American Federation of Labor was formed in December 1886 at a meeting of the Federation of Organized Trades and Labor Unions, giving more structure and potential power of organization to labor.

The conflict over dividing Rutland gained momentum through the 1880s and pitted local elites centered on the village against the marble elites in the outlying areas of Proctor and West Rutland. The division did not take place, however, until a new element entered local politics—the power of workers, in the marble industry and elsewhere.

The roots of worker politics went back to earlier labor conflicts in the quarries. As early as 1859, workers began to protest their working conditions. The first strike in the industry began on April 1, 1859, when about four hundred quarrymen who worked for four different marble companies went on strike to protest low wages and the poor housing conditions. They wanted one dollar per day in the summer, the peak season, and seventy-five cents in the winter when work was minimal. In a unified protest, they did not go back until June 1, after their demands were met.

At a time when many of the marble owners were paying their workers fifty cents per day, Barnes paid his workers substantially higher wages, one dollar per day. The workers respected Barnes and did not see him in the same light as they viewed the other owners. In this first marble strike, workers did not walk out of Barnes's quarry. When workers were forced from their company-owned rented shacks, Barnes, like Father Francis Picard, sought out shelters for the displaced workers, most of whom were Picard's parishioners. The support network for the workers, the division within the ranks of the marble owners, the united front of the workers and the pressure of the peak time for quarrying led to a successful conclusion of the strike two months later.

Barnes, one of the first to quarry marble in West Rutland and the most influential marble owner in the generation before Redfield Proctor, was more sympathetic to his workers than other marble owners. He permitted his workers to construct their own housing near the quarry. He also became a land developer and recycled the waste from the quarries, filling part of the swamp and then selling the land for building lots. Under his development, that section of town became the new dynamic growth area of the community.

The second major marble strike occurred during the Civil War in April 1864. Quarrymen sought $1.50 a day and a ten-hour workday. Companies offered $1.50 for an eleven-hour workday. John Cain, the editor of the *Rutland Courier*, supported the strikers. When both sides hardened their positions, the strike was inevitable. The workers struck against three of the four companies, all except Sheldon and Slason. On May 1, the Rutland Marble Company went to court to get an eviction order to force families from their company-rented houses. The *Rutland Herald* reported, "It is the intention of the Company to clear the tenements of their recent occupants and to employ new hands and resume work as soon as possible."[195] It was a frequent practice of the marble companies of the time to use the courts against the workers when workers struck.

In the spring of 1868, the workers struck again. Known to the workers as "the Big Turn Out," a reference to the workers being evicted from their rented homes, this strike was broken by the marble companies when they employed a new strategy. The Rutland Marble Company imported seventy-five French Canadians and their families to replace the strikers. The French Canadians were brought in by railroad from Montreal. Word of the marble company's plan spread quickly. When the train got close to West Rutland, the officials stopped the train, fearful that armed strikers and the new workers would confront one another. Despite such preventive measures, a brawl continued until the law officials arrived and made arrests.[196] For years afterward, memories of this incident continued to incite bitter feelings between the Irish and the French.

The fourth marble strike occurred in February 1880. At that time, marble companies in West Rutland informed their workers that they would pay $1.10 for an eleven-hour day. On March 1, the companies rescinded their promise and told the workers that they would pay $1.00 for a ten-hour day.

All of the quarrymen from the Rutland Marble Company and two-thirds at Sheldon and Sons—about two hundred workingmen—struck in support of a pay scale of $1.25 for a ten-hour day. The company stuck to its lower offer and refused to negotiate. It issued an ultimatum to the workers to return to work by Wednesday or vacate the company housing. There was a brief announcement in Thursday's *Rutland Daily Herald*: "The West Rutland quarrymen have all gone to work and the strike is over."[197]

By 1882, the marble business was booming, which meant an increased demand for workers.[198] In March 1882, there was a racial disturbance at the Columbian Mill that caused a minor strike. Twenty-five polishers quit work because an African American had just been hired "to do their work." The *Herald* went on to comment, "It is rather late in the day, particularly in Vermont, for men to object to working with a colored man, as these persons have found to their cost."[199] The disturbance affected only one division, the polishing department. In the rest of the mill there was no problem. The company supported the African American, and this minor strike collapsed.

A new labor solidarity was emerging in the 1880s, both at the national level and at the local level. Workers were joining more social and political organizations. The marble workers began to hold dances. At the first dance, the marble workers "danced away the greater part of the night." So successful was the event that it was proposed to be an annual event.[200] In 1881, nearly one hundred couples danced at the town hall with music from the opera house orchestra and a supper provided by the Berwick House, one of the premier hotels in the area.[201]

More importantly, the immigrants in the 1880s were seeking a public voice to challenge the system, unlike the earlier immigrants of the 1850s and 1860s, who had been marginalized in the public forum. At first, since the Republican Party was firmly in the hands of the marble elites, the only option for the opposition was to join the Democratic Party. Later, workers also found a public voice through the Knights of Labor, which organized chapters in Rutland and West Rutland.

In January 1886, J.J. Largan came from Boston to initiate candidates into the local Assembly of the Knights of Labor. A blindfolded reporter was escorted to the secret meeting. He was invited to the meeting so that the challenge to the old order would be known. The reporter from the *Herald* interviewed one of the Knights about the membership and objectives and was told:

We have been working in secret for we knew that if the suspicions of candidates were aroused before our organization was complete they would attempt to crush it out, and would probably have succeeded undoing it at first. But now that we are sure and have members in every department of labor in Rutland we have nothing to fear as we are strong enough to resist and maintain our independence. Yet the employers do not know now how many of their men have been initiated into the order and it is for our interest to keep quiet for awhile. No, the organization is not started to get on a strike. Workingmen here are pretty well satisfied now and the order endeavors to avoid strikes by arbitration whenever this can be done and still maintain the interest of the employee. We want Rutland capitalists, however, to recognize the organization, and we also want to help forward the cause all over the country, by sympathy with its principles and contributing funds when it is necessary to advance its interest. Our great object here at that will be to interest workingmen to movements for their betterment and there will probably be no call for violent measures.[202]

The possibility of an imminent strike in Rutland was a concern, especially when viewed in the context of what was happening nationally. In 1886 there were 1,432 strikes, and 55.3 percent of them were ordered by unions. In 1887, the number of strikes continued at approximately the same level, 1,436 strikes, but the union influence indicated a growing strength. Unions ordered 66.3 percent of the strikes in that year.[203]

In March 1886, the local of the Knights of Labor demanded that workers receive higher pay. The threat of a fifth strike was in the air. Labor and company officials met. The companies had prepared by stockpiling marble when there was little demand during the winter months. The company representatives also reminded labor of the increased number of potential workers. "The men," the *Herald* reported, "seem satisfied with the explanation of the companies."[204]

The workers now took a new tack. The Knights organized a united Labor Convention in Rutland. Quarryman and West Rutland master workman James Gillespie declared, "The time has come when we propose to have a hand in the legislation by which we are governed."[205] Knights Local Assembly 5160 offered a palpable threat to Rutland's political and economic establishment for the positions to be filled in the fall election on September 7, 1886.[206]

A new political alignment was starting to take place that began a decade earlier. In 1876, the Workingmen's Party of the United States was formed to deal with the rapid industrialization of the nation after the Civil War and particularly with the increasing shift toward unprecedented wealth for the new "captains of industry" at the expense of the worker.

In the United States, a group of socialists from around the country met in Philadelphia to assert workingmen's independence from the power of the capitalists. The ideas reflected trade union policies of the International Workingmen's Association, which had based its ideas on the contemporary analysis of Karl Marx. The confrontations and strikes added to the anxiety of the workers. Such concerns did not go unnoticed in the Marble Valley. Workers formed a chapter of the Workingmen's Party in Rutland.

In the summer, the caucus of the Workingmen's Party organized and selected its own candidates to run on the United Labor ticket.

The Workingmen's caucus in Rutland set out its agenda for reform:

> *We demand the repeal of the law known as the trustee process.*
> *We demand a bill obliging employers to pay their help weekly in cash.*
> *We demand the repeal of the law authorizing the board of civil authority to elect an overseer of the poor, and that he should be elected by the people.*
> *We demand a law to be known as the employer's liability act, to make employers liable for injuries received through carelessness or inefficiency of the employer or his agent.*
> *We demand the establishment of free evening schools for at least six months in every year in all towns over 7000 inhabitants.*
> *We demand a law making 10 hours a day's work.*[207]

C.M. Walker, a Republican and representative from Fair Haven (but not a Knight), wrote to the *Herald* in support of some of the demands of the Workingmen, especially the weekly wage and the trustee process. Monthly payment was a common practice, and often payments were delayed to the fifteenth or twentieth of the succeeding month. "So it is about six weeks from the time the poor laborer commences work before he receives a dollar of his earnings…I am rejoiced to learn that the laboring men at their late caucus have placed their foot on it and that your paper is taking high ground upon both subjects [weekly payments and trustee]."[208]

Some companies had paid in company script, and some had handed the workers' money over to an assigned trustee, as could occur with young workers, but the practice might perpetuate itself longer than was needed. To cover cost and risk, merchants and others would charge 10 to 15 percent more because workers would have to buy on credit. Aldace F. Walker, a lawyer and former president of the Vermont Bar Association, also wrote to the *Herald* in support of the Workingmen's demands. His overall assessment was that "the workingmen who composed the recent caucus, not only know what they want, but their demands are substantially right and just."[209]

The Workingmen's Party supported an Irish Catholic, James Hogan, as its candidate for representative to the state legislature. The son of an Irish quarryman, he had grown up in Rutland, worked in the quarries and was now a clothing store owner.

Redfield Proctor acknowledged the Workingmen but did not in any way support them. He reminded the electorate that the Republican Party had challenged the political process, noting Hogan's religion and ethnicity, as the first local Irish Catholic to run for high office, but asserting that the Republican Party had opened the political system to the "colored races in the first place."[210] To Proctor, the Republican Party provided a stable vehicle for developing the region. Further, the Grand Old Party was an extension of the Grand Army of the Republic, and citizens owed a political and social debt to the party.

The night before the election, the Workingmen rallied at the skating rink in the city in support of their candidates. In addition to the Workingmen in the town who could walk to the rally, other workers came in "a special train…from Sutherland Falls," and many also came in from Center and West Rutland; about one thousand attended in all.[211] As part of the get-out-the-vote, a special train left West Rutland at 3:30 a.m. to bring voters to the polls and returned when the voting was over. For the town election, the voting ballot was open from 9:00 a.m. to 3:00 p.m., and for the general election it was open from 9:00 a.m. to 5:00 p.m. The Vermont Marble Company closed the quarries, mills and shops to allow the workers to participate.[212]

On September 7, the town held the largest town meeting ever, and the citizens, many of them Knights, elected a full slate of independent labor candidates. It was a stunning victory and made the establishment apprehensive.[213] Hogan convincingly won the election as town representative with a vote of 1,645 out of 2,645 votes cast. His nearest competitor,

Republican H.A. Smith, garnered 744 votes, and Democrat G.J. Wardwell received 247. Not only had the Workingmen's Party candidate won, but their entire slate for justices beat the Republican and Democratic slates, as well.[214]

The *Rutland Herald* described the election as "Rutland's Quake" and blamed Democrats: "Some [of the blame for the result of the election] was republican, but most of it came from the democrats…Mr. Hogan, as we have said before, is a man of culture, good character and appearance, and will make a creditable member. He will have influence if he takes care to secure influential allies."[215] The *Herald* was impressed with the orderliness of the election. "Rutland never saw a more orderly election than that of yesterday," unlike what happened in the neighboring town of Mendon. The *Herald* went on to say, "If the workingmen will only conquer rum they can rule the world."[216]

The incident at Mendon contrasted with the decorum of the Rutland Workingmen's election. Before the meeting began in Mendon, twenty or thirty men were "conspicuously drunk," coming up the street from the house of the Democratic candidate Jerry C. Thornton. Two young men named Duffy verbally abused Republicans. One of the Duffy boys was knocked down, and a fight ensued. A messenger was sent to Rutland for the sheriff and the deputy sheriff. By the time the sheriffs arrived, the disturbance had quieted down and their friends had made the combatants presentable.[217] The *Herald* judged the attack to be deliberate by the Workingmen to influence the election. Even the Democrats were alarmed. "[I]t disgusted the respectable and sober democrats who would gladly have suppressed it, for the credit of the town, if they could."[218] The incident, while depicting the Mendon Knights in a bad light, did not overshadow the impressive behavior of the Rutland Knights' organization.

"Rutland's Quake" was a local manifestation of the "Great Upheaval" of 1886. In New York, Henry George as a mayoral candidate received more votes than Teddy Roosevelt, the Republican candidate for mayor. In 1879, George had first published *Progress and Poverty: An Inquiry into the Cause of Industrial Depressions and of Increase in Want with Increase of Wealth*. George was raising disturbing questions about the organization of society. His subtitle challenges the order of Andrew Carnegie's argument from calling for the voluntary redistribution of wealth in *The Gospel of Wealth* under a laissez-faire government to creating interventionist government with a power to tax—if land, for example, is not developed for public benefit rather than private profit.

Local Republicans worried that the unanticipated results of the election might lead to further unexpected ramifications. It was a crisis. The election sent shock waves to the pro-village folk who desired the town to become a city. Some of the elites in the business community feared "mob rule" by the working class and contemplated ways to hold on to power. One of these might be division of Rutland. On the blue-collar side of the tracks, some of the more radical workers were contemplating the division of the town to protect themselves. Both sides had their reasons for the division of the town.

One way for the Republicans to regain power was to remove the Workingmen from office. An attack on Hogan and attempt to remove him from office and discredit the Workingmen came just a week after the election. The opponents charged that he was ineligible to run for office because he did not fulfill the one-year residency requirement, since he had been away. He had left Rutland for St. Johnsbury on July 4, 1884, married at Swanton in September of that year and returned to Rutland in November 1885. Hogan's position was that his residency was in Rutland. He voted only in Rutland and was on the voter checklist only in Rutland and nowhere else.[219]

The *Herald* sounded a warning to the Knights:

> [While] *the marble quarries are here as stable and inexhaustible as the mountains* [n]*o conditions of population or interference of labor agitation can remove the source of supply, and the iron market cannot materially affect the cost of production…there is one contingency, however, on which the stable marble industry depends, and that is the tariff. Reduce this and Rutland's prosperity is checked, and remove it entirely and her growth will come to a standstill.*[220]

One of the national issues the Knights were discussing was the removal of protective tariffs. The *Herald* also noted how easily a "manufacturer of fabrics" could leave a village, "leaving the factory deserted and the village to suffer by the loss."[221]

Advocates for separation representing the rural interests summed up their bid for economic, moral and local control in their slogan for separation from the village: "Prosperity, temperance, and good government." In early November, the advocates for division again presented their arguments before the legislature:

Proctor will have nearly ten and one-half square miles—a larger area than Burlington, Montpelier, Vergennes, Landgrove and several other towns. It will have about 1,724 inhabitants—a number in excess of about one hundred and ninety other towns in the State…The schools…are excellent; the roads, the best in that section; the village hall, school houses, churches, public library, the general appearance of the village, and its character for good order…are such that it may be fairly called a model village. All of the voters of the village of Proctor, except three; all of the farmers in that part of District No. 10, to be annexed, except one; and all of the voters in that part of Pittsford included in the proposed town have expressed such a wish.

Therefore it may be regarded as conclusively established, that Proctor has all the elements of a prosperous, well governed and harmonious town, amply capable of taking care of itself, and better able to secure for itself prosperity, temperance and general good government tha[n] it would be under the guardianship of any other municipality.

Their local interests and government would be in their own hands instead of being centered in a much larger village, where the majority of the voters are not familiar with their wants and needs…

It would promote public improvement, remove unpleasant differences, preserve the town system of government to a considerable people unwilling to be taken into a city.[222]

Many in the business community of the village wanted to regain power and to hold on to the outlying districts for their financial support of the village. General W.Y.W. Ripley recalled a town meeting about pleas to erect Memorial Hall in the village as a tribute to the Marble Valley's Civil War volunteers and a concern that village forces were using the proposed memorial building as leverage against West Rutland's possible secession. If West Rutland persisted in its plans to separate from the town, anti-division proponents vindictively threatened to penalize West Rutland by increasing the size of the memorial building and obligating West Rutland to pay more. West Rutland already felt that its taxes were going for improvements such as roads in the village rather than in the outlying districts and that this threat of an increased assessment for the war memorial would be another blatant example of power unfairly exercised by the village.[223]

The rivalry between Proctor, an advocate of division, and Clement, an anti-division proponent, became more pronounced when Proctor used his influence in the state legislature to support the 1886 proposal to separate Sutherland Falls and West Rutland from Rutland. By doing so, Proctor, who had his own agenda, was also supporting the workers' agenda. By 1886, P.W. Clement, as Percival was frequently called, used the *Rutland Daily Herald* to fight what he saw as Proctor's proposed 1886 Rutland division. P.W. wrote a number of "letters to the editor" under a pseudonym, suggesting that Proctor influenced his workmen to petition for and vote for the split. In a letter to the editor on November 2, 1886, Clement, under a pseudonym, wrote:

> *To Mr. Proctor (for Mr. is his proper name, by the way, not governor) all this excitement and running to Montpelier indicates a panicky state of feeling, which must be very gratifying to his vanity when he reflects that he is the prime cause of it all. The ex-governor's reasons for "secession" are said to be: 1st, an ambitious desire for fame; 2nd to divide and break the power of the Knights of Labor; 3rd, to create an office and then fill in; in fact, to establish a sort of primogeniture system in regard to the office of representative, for the exclusive benefit of the Proctor family and their descendants. If these impressions are the result of careless observations and are wrong, I would gladly stand corrected when proper proof is presented that they are wrong…A man starting out for fame may have to be content with acquiring notoriety; dividing the Knights of Labor is a thankless task; it is like cutting water with a knife; and the idea of a man seeking to divide a town for personal reasons and benefits is somewhat like using a cannon to shoot a sparrow; it is in fact an exaggerated case of the tail trying to wag the dog…Rutland will not consent to be dictated to or be overruled by the small hamlet of Proctor…*
>
> *(signed) Fabricus*[224]

There was also concern that the Proctor family would own 97 percent of the property of the newly separated town, creating a private political and economic fiefdom with inordinate political power.[225] Indeed, when the town was separated from Rutland Village, Redfield Proctor served as the representative to the state legislature, his son Fletcher was the school commissioner and most of the town officers also worked for the Vermont Marble Company.

Clement's use of the newspaper for self-serving purposes outweighed his interest in its financial success. An old battle erupted over whether the village—that is, the urban center of Rutland Town—should be formally incorporated as a city. The status of the village as a city would contrast with the towns and give preeminence to the village. It would also establish a new form of government, with the principal and influential leader being a mayor. P.W. Clement was now instrumental in formulating the Rutland City Charter and used the *Rutland Daily Herald* to advance the drive. The city formation movement confirmed a special status to Rutland as a vibrant center of political and business activity and added to the political and social tension in the area. Sutherland Falls/Proctor and West Rutland saw Rutland Village as the common enemy, and therefore the advocates of division asked for the separation of West Rutland as well.

Marble workers were also asked their opinion. When asked before the legislature's investigation committee, P.J. Dunnigan, a stonecutter, on November 2, 1886, voiced the concerns of many of the workers, who viewed the issue in geographic, economic and political terms:

> *Q: You think a majority want to be set off from East Rutland?*
> *A: Yes, sir: we have to go up there to do all our business. Go up there to vote, for town clerk, for bank business. Think we would have a bank here of our own if we had a town of our own.*[8]

Other testifiers stated that the housing in Proctor and West Rutland was more than adequate, that the schools were adequate and that both communities were orderly and self-sufficient.

On Thursday, November 18, 1886, legislation passed, making Proctor a separate town, and on the following day, Friday, November 19, 1886, West Rutland was also made a separate town, bypassing the village stage. Thus, in 1886, the former Rutland town was divided into four separate legal entities: Proctor, West Rutland, Rutland Town and Rutland Village.[227]

The vote on the incorporation of Proctor demonstrated the political power of Redfield Proctor. The legislature dealt with the incorporation of Proctor before West Rutland and the vote in the Senate, where Redfield Proctor had personal and political power, contrasted dramatically with the House vote. The vote in the House for incorporation of Proctor was 128 to 91. In the Senate it was 27 to 0. On the following day, November 19, the legislature passed Act 138 for the division of West Rutland. The vote in the House on this bill was 119 to 101; the vote in the Senate was 27 to 1.[228]

The division of Rutland into Rutland Village, West Rutland, Proctor and Rutland Town now added another dimension to the quest for power. The Republicans saw a way of regaining power and dislodging the Workingmen, who had triumphed in September 1886.

Before the end of the year, the legislature voided the September 1886 elections, stripping Hogan of his position as state legislator and removing all fifteen United Labor justices of the peace.[229] The rationale of the legislature was that the election of the candidates took place before the division of Rutland, and now that it was divided, the representatives did not fairly represent their new constituencies.

In addition, the legislature required elected officials from the divided towns to post a bond of $1,000 to $5,000. This effectively blocked workers from running for office, since they had little available wealth on which to draw on such short notice. The response of the Workingmen was to increase their political activities, and they set forth their plans for the March 1887 elections.

To the workers, the division redoubled their efforts. Potentially, they could organize more effectively in smaller geographic areas. By the end of the year, there were four chapters of the Knights, two of them in West Rutland, indicating that the marble workers sought their own voice to address issues. The blatant attempt by the fearful elite to control the situation, and the voiding of the September elections, only angered labor more. In February 1887, the Workingmen placed a notice in the paper:

> *Workingmen!*
> *You are hereby requested to appear at the Town Hall on Monday evening at 8 o'clock p.m., sharp, to put in nomination suitable persons for town offices for the ensuing year.*
> *(signed) Workingmen's Town Committee*[230]

The Workingmen's ticket submitted a full slate of candidates for Rutland Village. They came from a variety of occupations. Charles Clark and Henry F. Field were tellers and cashiers at local banks. Frank H. Welch was a marble cutter, and Edward Richard Ryan was a marble polisher.

Joseph Austin and Edward Duffy were blacksmiths. Patrick Keenan, Arthur G. Fuller, Edgar K. Davis and John Noble Bryan McKean were farmers. Henry Austin and John A. Huffmire were machinists. George H. Cheney and William H. Owen were general merchandisers. James A. Merrill, law student, was the Workingmen's candidate for superintendent of schools. There was also a carpenter, a proprietor of a livery house and a flour and grain seller.[231]

The Workingmen's Resolution Committee set out its agenda:

We Demand:
Economical administration of town affairs.
Strict account of all public transactions and rendered also as to be perfectly understood.
Just and equitable taxation.
All work on roads to be done in a thorough and permanent manner.
We condemn the practice of selectmen or other town officers employing themselves in the performance of work outside of their regular duties.
We demand that grand juror or other officers of the law shall not debase their offices to extent of levying blackmail on offenders, but shall conform absolutely to the law.
We recommend that three per cent of the grand list be raised for the benefit of the public library, of which two per cent shall be used for the purchase of books.[232]

The opposition to the Workingmen called itself the Citizens' Party, a euphemistic name obscuring the fact that it was an appeal to Democrats and Republicans to join together to stop the worker offensive. The Citizens' Party exploited the issue of secrecy and class. The Citizens' Party warned voters about a possible disaster if the Workingmen won, accusing the Workingmen of forming a cabal and engaging in a conspiracy:

Citizens' Ticket
The Ticket That Has Not Been Prepared by a Secret Society and Ratified in Public, But Which Some of the Most Substantial Citizens of all Parties and Classes Have United Upon and Which Every Voter Who Loves and Would Preserve His Town Should Turn out and Support.[233]

In March 1887, the Knights of Labor candidates with their unified support won all the local offices, stunning the Citizens' Party, which had spread fear and uncertainty to blunt the threat. The Knights also won beyond Rutland in other places in the Marble Valley, such as West Rutland, Brandon, Fair Haven and Danby. P.W. Clement interpreted the result as the victory of a class unfit to rule—or, at least, one with little experience in governing. Only disaster would result: "Another dangerous feature…is that the officers elected are so largely from one class of inhabitants and so unfamiliar with public affairs."[234]

At the town meeting on March 2, 1887, Labor voted for a new town school system, replacing the district school, and on March 10, the new school directors assumed their positions. Louis Walker represented District 2 on the board; the *Herald* stated that he had "no experience in school matter or other public duties. He is 30 years old and a man of ordinary capacity and intelligence."[235] Another member was Joseph Austin, a blacksmith and like the others a member of the Knights of Labor. The *Herald* admitted that he was "an intelligent and fairly educated man of very positive opinions…[who] believes in liberal education and the expenditures of all money to establish creditable schools."[236] Better schools were one of the main objectives of the Workingmen. Education was seen as the way to economic success, and good schools, whether public or parochial, were a prime concern of the immigrant and the worker. Five hundred citizens attended the first school board meeting in Rutland after the division, many of them members of the Knights of Labor.

Some feared that the new board would spend too much money. Such expenditures would be going to support foreigners by excessive spending for construction of public schools. Referring to the Knights of Labor, one participant at the meeting stated, "It has taken control of town meetings and of schools."[237] The new system provided more local control and participation. Some of the schools in West Rutland and Rutland were in deplorable condition. Now that the pro-worker school board had secured key positions, they began a building campaign. Even before the breakup of Rutland, there had been a strong movement for new schools to serve immigrants. For instance, the West Rutland English and Classical High School opened in 1881.

In Rutland after the division, the United Labor candidates, the name the Workingmen used, went on a building spree to support the burgeoning immigrant worker population. At 30 Pine Street, Kingsley School was built in 1888 to the latest standards at the cost of $12,285. The Longfellow School was constructed in 1890 at a cost of $25,000, and others followed: the Watkins School in 1892, the Lincoln School in 1895 and the Park Street School in 1897. Within a span of ten years, Rutland acquired five modern schools. School construction continued under successive administrations, even when Labor was in the minority and even during the severest depression of the century. Labor had stressed the importance of education in an increasingly industrial age that demanded more skills. In an effort to provide a more activist government in support of its citizens, the town meeting also mandated public funding to the Rutland Library to create a free lending library.[238]

The business elite criticized Labor through 1887 and berated citizens who did not vote. The *Herald* kept up its attack on Labor by arguing that it represented just a small group. To make sure the patriotic and good citizens voted next time, the *Herald* printed a list of voters who did not vote "and let the Knights of Labor carry the town."[239] The *Herald* decried the seeming disorder of the village meeting. "There are more than 1600 names on the check list. Only 1168 men voted. Last [election] 1256 voted, so we are growing worse instead of better. Saturday the *Herald* will print the names of those who did not vote."[240] It published the names again. From the *Herald*'s viewpoint, a small, dedicated special interest group of Knights had usurped the election. If more citizens had voted, it reasoned, the Knights would not have won.

The Knights included many immigrant workers, including Italians, Irish and French Canadians. The argument of nativism had been used successfully in the past as a scare tactic in the valley and in the state, and it could be used again. Vermont's U.S. senator Justin Morrill in 1887, for instance, expressed fears that immigrants would affect "the future character of the American people…republican institutions, higher wages, land homesteads, [and] universal education." The threat came from the new immigration from southern and eastern Europe. Southern and eastern Europeans bore "the mark of Cain" and comprised a class of "outcasts and criminals…imbeciles, idiots, and lunatics."[241] In 1887, a writer to the *Herald* bemoaned the impact of foreigners: "[There is] no guarantee that ignorant Italians, anarchists, and infidels cannot and will not control the town meeting and as a result all the schools in the town."[242]

This time the Citizens' Party also frightened voters with the additional prospect that, if Labor Party candidates won, businesses would move out of Rutland and plunge the community into a terrible economic panic. The loss of a Rutland shirt factory when it moved out of state in early 1888 was blamed on the Labor Party and seemed to lend credibility to the Citizens' Party prediction of more losses. Anxiety and rumors mounted that other companies might also leave. In fact, the Howe Scale Company, soon to become one of the largest Rutland employers, reorganized and moved from Brandon to Rutland, but the anxiety still persisted.

When voters met in Rutland's town meeting in March 1888, the signal that the Citizens' Party might win came early in the evening when Judge Veazey—Republican, member of the elite and former business partner of Redfield Proctor—was selected by ballot for village moderator with a 113 majority.[243]

The *Herald* announced the election results on its front page with large, bold headlines:

RUTLAND REDEEMED!
One Year of Class Government Thought Enough
Citizens' Candidates Elected by a Rousing Majority
The Verdict of the Voters Given for Good Government
Practical Men and Non-Partisan Administration Endorsed
West Rutland and Brandon Wheel into the Column of Reform[244]

The *Herald* sounded the theme of moral redemption and good business practices in its victory celebration in its columns.[245] "The town is redeemed from the bad repute and costly and inefficient control of last year and its affairs are now placed in charge of some of the ablest and best known men."[246] Even West Rutland and Brandon, strongholds of Labor in the previous election, had gone over to the Citizens' Party.

Despite the *Herald*'s triumphant extolling of the Citizens' Party's victory and near sweep of the election (one Labor candidate did win), the election was closer than the *Herald* headlines led readers to believe. The close tabulation did not finish until four o'clock in the morning, when the Citizens' Party was finally declared the winner.

In this tense atmosphere, Levi Kingsley, a Civil War veteran, former freight handler and now a merchant, was the only candidate sympathetic to Labor to win town office in 1888. The *Herald*, on Thursday, reassured its readers that Kingsley had much more in common with the Citizens' Party than he did with Labor. He was, after all, a prominent merchant, a village president in 1886 and a captain of the Steamer Company. In the *Herald*'s reassuring voice, "General Levi Kingsley was elected on the workingmen's ticket, but in no way is he associated with that clique."[217]

CHAPTER 7

THE STRUGGLE FOR CONTROL

1888–1900

The sense of place, and its underlying paramount issue of security, had seemed to be resolved when the geographically unified town of Rutland had fragmented into four separate areas: Proctor, Rutland Village, West Rutland and the remaining Rutland Town. The village of Proctor was safely under the control of the Vermont Marble Company and the Proctors; many marble workers lived in the larger area of West Rutland. Rutland Village, the railway hub, was the financial center, where many marble workers also lived.

The identification with place—and the neighborhood and the churches—intensified a sense of common values. For instance, the Irish in West Rutland lived near and went to church at St. Bridget's, built by the marble workers' volunteer labor with stone donated by a local marble company. The Irish in Rutland went to Christ the King Church, another church constructed of marble and which was in the process of building a school. In the gut (short for "gutter"), St. Peter's, built earlier by the Irish, was now becoming an active social center for the growing Italian community. In Rutland was the Immaculate Heart of Mary Church, a center for French Catholics; there was also the Sacred Heart of Jesus, a French church in West Rutland. A Polish church in West Rutland would join the other ethnically oriented churches in 1905. Most of the marble and financial elites attended the Grace Congregational Church or Trinity Episcopal Church, the latter also constructed of marble. Out of these social, geographic and economic conclaves, other issues could now be addressed. The various groups simultaneously acted defensively and assertively.

The Proctor Company Store was far more than a mere grocery store. It performed many of the functions of a post office, a bank, a jeweler and a furniture store. *Courtesy of Vermont Marble Museum.*

The West Rutland Company Store has a new role as the base for the internationally recognized Carving Studio and Sculpture Center. *Mike Austin Collection.*

A former storefront in West Rutland now serves as gallery space for the Carving Studio. *Mike Austin Collection.*

West Rutland School's original building was constructed of white marble blocks very similar to the Proctor High School. The schools are friendly athletic rivals. *Mike Austin Collection.*

Marble Bank on West Street in Rutland epitomizes the Italianate-style architecture popular when it was built. At the top of the bank its name is inscribed; because of the amount of marble in the area, the locale became known as the Marble City. *Mike Austin Collection.*

In 1888, the elites within the Republican and Democrat establishments drew more closely together because of the threat of further worker radicalization. As workers had discovered, if their public voice was to be heard, it would have to be heard outside the two-party system. The Democrats had taken the worker voice so far, but they had compromised as they gained power. So comfortable was that arrangement between Democrats and Republicans in Rutland and West Rutland that in 1884, for example, before the extraordinary events of 1887 when the Workingmen swept the elections, they offered an identical slate, with one exception: L.W. Redington of Rutland, an attorney and a Democrat, was Republican enough in his social connections to pose no serious threat to the existing political arrangement.[248]

Most political leaders in Vermont traveled in a small social circle. Social, business and political circles intersected. Most in the inner circle of power

Proctor School continues to serve its community and even to this day benefits from the Proctor family largesse via scholarships. The high school in its style is similar to its rival West Rutland School. *Mike Austin Collection.*

belonged to mainline Protestant churches, and most often that meant, for Rutland, the Episcopal or Congregational Church. They frequently also belonged to the Masonic Lodge or Elks Club.

Redfield Proctor remained the most powerful member of the ruling elite. After the division of Rutland in 1886, Proctor was again a member of the House, being the first representative from the new town of Proctor; at that session he served as chairman of the powerful Committee on Ways and Means. At the state and national level, Proctor prospered as Vermont solidified its identity with the Republican Party.

At the Republican National Convention in Chicago in June 1888, former governor Proctor was the chairman of the Vermont delegation. Proctor played a prominent role in helping secure the nomination for Benjamin Harrison by keeping Vermont's delegation unanimously in support of him from the beginning, and Vermont was the only state to cast its entire vote for Harrison on every ballot. At the October session, the Vermont legislature adopted a joint resolution urging Proctor's appointment for a cabinet position, and on March 5, 1889, President Harrison appointed him secretary of war.[219] When he was so appointed, Proctor ended active connection with Vermont Marble Company, and his son, Fletcher Proctor, at age twenty-nine, took over the company. Fletcher remained president of Vermont Marble Company until his death in 1911.

To discredit the Workingmen in Rutland, both the Democrats and Republicans used scare tactics, claiming that the local economy would be hurt if the Workingmen were elected to office again. Belying these scare tactics, economic growth in Rutland was actually continuing. The Howe Scale Company moved from Brandon to Rutland in 1888, with John Mead as its president. The Vermont School Seat Company was founded in the town. Mosely and Stoddard, a cheese and butter manufacturer, moved from Poultney to 12 Forest Street in Rutland in 1890. The Chase Toy Factory moved from Mount Holly to Curtis Avenue in Rutland. With financial help from George Chaffee, F.R. Patch of Proctor established the F.R. Patch Company, later known as Patch-Wagner, a maker and supplier of marble cutting and finishing equipment, which eventually developed a national and international market. The Marble City Electric Company challenged the Rutland Gas Company for dominance in lighting the city and supplying power. The combination of a skilled labor force, a railroad terminal and a growing cluster of business had fostered this growth.[250]

By 1890, Rutland was being touted as a place at the cutting edge of progress. Here, according to a promotional book on industry, was the place to come, a place in which to invest:

> *The place* [Rutland] *presents all the attractive appearances of a live and wide awake New England centre. The streets are brilliantly lighted with the electric light, and there are two electric light plants. There is a complete telephone system, district messenger service, a vigilant fire department, free mail delivery, public library, Y.M.C.A. building, many social organizations. Masonic and other secret society lodges, a fine opera house, and indeed everything calculated to make a residence here pleasant and agreeable.*[251]

By 1894, the Rutland Street Railway Company, organized in 1882 with horse-drawn cars, now used the new electric energy to develop connections as far as Plain, Granger, South, Forest and West Streets. The Bardwell, the Bates, the Berwick and the new Hamilton hotels were constructed close to the railroad depot; all had rooms for single male working boarders.

The promotional report noted the transportation and other improvements and cited the primacy of marble to the region, again emphasizing the potential for future investment:

Rutland is also a great marble centre, its citizens and capitalists being interested in quarries and mills in various parts of the State. Taking the town proper, of West and Centre Rutland, and Proctor all of which if not suburbs, are in intimate contiguity to Rutland, the production of marble here probably amounts to nearly half of the entire product of the United States. In addition marble quarrying and working machinery is produced here.[252]

The owners and managers of these enterprises, however, saw danger in the successes of worker politics. They railed, in particular, at the newer immigrants who worked in the quarries and the factories. As governor in 1888, William Dillingham echoed the nativist strand in Vermont and Rutland when he addressed the legislature at the beginning of the session. "The laws for the encouragement of virtue and the prevention of vice and immorality ought to be kept constantly in force."[253] For him, economic failure was a consequence of moral failure and mental instability associated with the new immigrants. It was fertile ground for the eugenics movement, which Vermont would soon embrace.[254]

Dillingham urged action to combat this alleged threat to the native population. He expanded the state mental hospital system and built a mental hospital in Waterbury in 1891 in addition to the existing one at Brattleboro. He strengthened the prohibition laws, advocating imprisonment for violators, who were assumed to be unruly Irish Catholics. The French were not exempt, either. Rowland Robinson, a Vermont author, wrote in 1892 that Catholic French Canadians were an "inferior class" with an innate disposition toward theft and whose "fingers were as light as their hearts"; Robinson also asserted that marriage with Vermont's Anglo-Saxons would corrupt indigenous values and result in "litters of filthy brats."[255] In 1890, when Dillingham was finishing his term as governor, he warned his fellow citizens again about the increasing number of undesirable foreigners in the state and the potential of radicalism they brought with them.[256] Dillingham was willing to make an exception for the Swedes, who contributed, he said, "a great and lasting benefit to the State."[257]

Dillingham continued his campaign against "undesirable foreigners" when he became a United States senator from Vermont in 1900. The four-year study he led reported in 1911 that southern and eastern Europeans were biologically inferior and that Scandinavians were the "purest" type —

99 percent Protestant, with the lowest rate of illiteracy; they made "ideal farmers and…Americanize more rapidly than other peoples."[258] Under the cloak of "scientific methodology," the commission relayed findings that the southern and eastern Europeans caused problems for employers and local officials and drove down wages for "native" Americans and older immigrant employees.[259]

In September 1892, the Democrats and the Workingmen allied in an attempt to gain further ground, but to no avail. P.W. Clement again ran in this election for representative as a Republican. Seneca M. Dorr, an investment banker and Democrat, opposed Clement and received the votes of the Workingmen. The polls opened at 9:00 a.m. and closed at 3:00 p.m., but there were still large lines, so the voting was extended. The first results were announced at 5:00 p.m., but there was no majority of votes cast for any one candidate, so the vote was opened again. Names of the voters were written down, and those who had not voted were sent for, as in the previous election. Finally at ten o'clock the next morning, Clement was declared the winner over Dorr, 1,242 votes to 1,173. Will Davis, a prohibitionist, received 28 votes. Some of the party operatives had been at the polls for thirty hours.

In 1892, the old guard leaders of the downtown section of Rutland, still growing with the rise of the railroads and its proximity to marble industry, resumed their agitation to incorporate the village as a city. That year, Clement bought the *Rutland Daily Herald* outright. Through his paper, Clement could lobby the legislature for the village to become a city. In a city form of government, a mayor and council would replace the town meeting. The senator from Rutland County, John A. Mead, president of the Howe Scale Company, worked with Clement in the House to secure a city charter for the village of Rutland. However, the representative of West Rutland, upset over the proposed boundaries of the city, offered an amendment that "culminated in a pitched battle in the House." Clement argued in favor of city status for Rutland: "Rutland had outgrown the town government and agitation for a city charter had been constant since 1886." After a drawn-out debate, the House rejected any amendments by a vote of 111 to 87. The House then passed the bill for incorporation, "Viva voce."[260] The bill then went to the governor for his signature.

On Monday, the *Rutland Daily Herald* for October 21, 1892, wrote in large type:

RUTLAND
BECAME A CITY SATURDAY
At 2:30 o'clock in the Afternoon
As Gov. Fuller Put his Signature to the Charter
The Bill was Passed by the Senate
Without any Debate
Or a Single Word of Opposition
And Was Then Hurried to the Governor,
But He Waited
Until the Hands of the Clock Reached 2:30
Then He Wrote on the Margin,
"Approved, Levi K. Fuller"[261]

The new city government formally separated and strengthened the executive branch. With the new city government, there were more taxes but also more services provided. A city-wide race elected the mayor, while aldermen were each elected by their individual wards. There were eleven wards, and one alderman was elected the president of the board. Within the executive branch were the city treasurer, the city attorney, the city grand juror, the city constable, the superintendent of streets, the superintendent of water, the city engineer, the chief of police, the overseer of the poor, the city physician, a board of health, cemetery commissioners, park commissioners, the inspector of lumber, the inspector of weights and measurers, the inspector of food, the inspector of buildings, the city weigher, assessors, auditors and commissioners of sinking funds.[262]

The new form of government distanced itself from the worker. Gone was the New England town meeting at which the citizens could assemble and challenge in open forum the issues or the candidates. Now the Australian ballot could quietly isolate the citizen in the progressive name of efficiency and convenience. Workers needed to join together and educate themselves on the best candidates to represent them.

The first mayor of the newly chartered city was former state senator John A. Mead. As a great-grandson of the first settler of Rutland, he had deep roots extending back into Rutland's early history. Mead was part of the network of elites concerned about stability and order and wary of threats to the political and social order. His connections bridged the important families in the area, including both the Clements and the Proctors. Workers tried to influence the new city government through a new Central Trades and Labor Council, which supported two winning candidates for the city council.

Just as Rutlanders were entering a new era as a city with a sense of optimism, the nation was plunged into a depression. A financial panic began in the last ten days of President Harrison's term, when the Philadelphia and Reading Railroad went bankrupt. President Cleveland, a Democrat, was sworn into office in March 1893, and shortly thereafter the panic spread to Wall Street. To protect themselves, banks called in their loans. Credit was scarce and businesses began to fail. By the end of the year, the panic had evolved into the worst depression that the nation had yet faced. For eight more years, the nation coped. From 1894 to 1898, the national unemployment rate stayed over 10 percent.[263]

The depression affected Rutland as it struggled through its first year as a city. The *Herald* reported: "Men Out of Work: Hundreds of Unwilling Idlers in the City."

The Citizens' Party, originally formed as a conservative coalition of Republicans, Democrats and United Workingmen, began to fall apart. Republicans feared that the Citizens' Party would lean toward worker interests to the detriment of their own. Local Democrats and Republicans returned to the traditional lines of self-interest and self-preservation.

Workers responded in a variety of ways. As early as September 21, 1892, twenty-five men met to found the Socialist Labor Club at the Brunswick House in Rutland on September 21, 1892. They set out thirteen objectives. The *Herald* printed most of the list:

- *Reduction of the hours of labor in proportion to the progress of production.*
- *The United States shall obtain possession of the railroads, canals, telegraphs, telephones and other means of public transportation and communication.*
- *The municipalities to obtain possession of the local railroads, ferries, water works, gas works, electric plants, and all industries requiring municipal franchises.*
- *The public lands to be declared inalienable. Revocation of all land grants to corporations or individuals, the conditions of which have not been complied with.*
- *Legal incorporations by the states of local trade unions which have no national organization.*

- *The United States to have exclusive right to issue money…*
- *School education of all children under 14 years of age to be compulsory, gratuitous, and accessible to all by public assistance in meals, clothing, books etc. where necessary.*
- *Repeal of all paupery, tramp, conspiracy, and sumptuary laws.*
- *Unabridged right of combination.*
- *Official statistics concerning the condition of labor. Prohibition of the employment of children of school age and of the employment of female labor in occupations detrimental to health or morality. Abolition of convict labor contract system.*
- *All wages to be paid in lawful money.*[264]

Distrustful of the two-party system, workers again organized a public voice that expressed their concerns—the Workingmen's Party. On July 5, 1893, the *Rutland Daily Herald* reported on "A People's Party: Organization in a State Convention held in Rutland." The state convention of the "people's party" was held on the deliberately symbolic date of July 4 at the Bardwell House, a prosperous hotel on Merchants Row where the Marble Princes held meetings and lodged.

The *Rutland Daily Herald* reported:

> *Our grandfathers owned their farms and homes but their grandsons do not. I believe the banks and railroad corporations have deprived us of them. We must strike at monopoly, and organize a third party for that purpose. We must repeal the blue laws of the state.*[265]

The Workingmen's Party was in sympathy with several of the key issues expressed nationally in the previous year by the Populists at their convention in the summer of 1892 and issued on the Fourth of July in what was called the Omaha Platform.

The clarion call trumpeted from the Midwest and the South found a responsive chord in the workers of the Marble Valley. The Omaha Platform of 1892 added a worker voice to the national dialogue on nativism. In their resolves, the Populists stated:

> *That we condemn the fallacy of protecting American labor under the present system, which opens our ports to the pauper and criminal cases of*

*the world, and crowds out our wage earners; and we denounce the present
ineffective laws against contract labor, and demand the further restriction of
undesirable immigration.*[266]

In July 1893, District Master Workman Drury "urged Vermont workers to
organize for political action in 1894."[267] Given the financial panic of 1893,
the workers were more inclined to elect one of their own as mayor, someone
who might be more sympathetic to their plight, rather than another person
from the business elite. The Republican ticket swept the entire election.[268]
The *Herald* also noted a change in the labor stronghold of West Rutland,
with the victory of all the Republican candidates, for "the first time in the
history of the town."[269]

The Rutland City Council representatives of labor responded to the
financial crisis. The labor advocates pushed for short-term public projects
like street grading and landscaping, which would benefit labor and promote
civic pride. The Republican-dominated city council, however, opposed local
work relief, labeling it "Tammany charity."[270] Not entirely unsympathetic to
labor's financial distress, the Republican elites believed in voluntary charity
rather than governmental intervention.

The *Herald* made a plea and organized a drive for soap and clothing to
distribute to needy children, and the paper also provided a special section for
men who were looking for work. A Women's Exchange was set up at which
"any intelligent [women] who are not and never can be artists, but who,
when changed circumstances and common sense demand that they shall
help themselves, have the wisdom to do what they can do well."[271]

The patronizing attitude of the elites added to the frustration of the
workers. The Republican elites controlled government, and their solutions
seemed inadequate and paltry. As the severe depression continued in 1894
and 1895, the winters were particularly hard on marble workers. The
quarries were shut down, and the workers were uncertain of how long the
depression would continue with no callbacks in the spring and summer.

In 1895, Republicans selected John Alexander Sheldon (1839–1910) as
their candidate for mayor. He had been a co-owner of the Sheldon and
Slason Marble Company. He had served in the Civil War with W.Y.W. Ripley,
also from a marble family. With his Civil War and marble connections,
Sheldon became a selectman of Rutland for three years, a trustee of the
village of Rutland for two years and president of the village board for one

year. When the village was incorporated as a city in 1893, he was chosen as an alderman and served for two years. As in the election of 1894, John D. Spellman, who was sympathetic to labor, ran as an Independent. Sheldon, however, brought in 200 more votes than Spellman (1,098 to 863), while labor candidate Alanson A. Orcutt, formerly of West Fort Ann, New York, and by trade a carriage painter, ran a poor third, with a total of 48 votes.[272] The financial situation hovered over the city like a dismal winter day, and Sheldon's election did nothing to improve it.

In March 1896, the workers and Democrats united in their opposition to the Republicans. Their support coalesced around a popular Democrat who was sympathetic to labor, Ward Seven alderman Thomas R. Browne (1859–1931). Browne was a former Knights of Labor organizer. With this combined support of labor and a more mainline party, Browne won the mayoral race.[273] Labor now seemed to be in a position to make progress on its agenda in these troubled times. Browne served from March 1896 to March 1897.[274] Although he became mayor, the Republicans still maintained the majority on the council.

The Moon Brook sewer project caused further tension. The Republican-dominated board was not willing to modify its resolution that the mayor had suggested, and again the board failed to override the mayor's veto. Two weeks later, on October 5, the mayor returned the resolution without comment.[275] A week later, at the next aldermen's meeting, the Moon Brook project became even more embarrassing for the aldermen. Three-fourths of the sewer pipes that had already been purchased were found to be faulty because the pipe "did not come up to specifications."[276] By the end of October, the legislative and executive branches of the city were in such a deadlock that a petition was circulating to amend the city charter, allowing the voters to choose the city engineer, the superintendent of streets and the superintendent of water works directly, bypassing the aldermen and the mayor. According to the *Herald*, "Several hundred signatures have been obtained and the petition will be forwarded to Montpelier."[277]

By November, the relationship between the mayor and the board had deteriorated into a bitter stalemate. The *Herald* commented on the board meeting of November 16: "The board of aldermen was in session last evening until nearly midnight and did not accomplish a great deal during the time."[278] The board had privately authorized work on Woodstock Avenue. "Mayor Browne gave the board a raking over in respect to certain bills that he refused to sign, stating that he had no authority to do so. The mayor said that the improvement on Woodstock avenue had not been authorized and that they had far exceeded the appropriations."[279] He went on to complain to the board about its action, saying that "he did not propose to get over the line to help the board of aldermen out of their trouble."[280]

The elite of Rutland faced the uncomfortable fact that Labor forces, in the midst of the crisis, had the greatest influence in the executive office of the city government. There was no telling what might happen in the future with Browne in office, reasoned the opposition. By the first week of February, several Republican names had been floated for election, including W.C. Landon, J.N. Woodfin and H.A. Sawyer, chair of the aldermanic board.[281] Several aldermen decided not to run for reelection. Six of the eleven aldermanic seats became vacant that year. W.F. Burditt, H.A. Sawyer, A.S. Fuller, George Royce, G.C. Thrall and E.B. Aldrich, all part of the moneyed interests of Rutland and all opposed to Mayor Browne, were willing to run for reelection. "There is," noted the *Herald*, "more politics per square inch now in various wards than for a long time past."[282]

In this crisis, the business community decided to back a single candidate so as not to divide the field. An open letter from the city chair of the Republican Party, signed by prominent Republicans in the city, was sent to Percival Clement asking him to run for mayor. Clement replied on February 11 to them in the *Herald*:

> *In reply to your request that I be a candidate for office of mayor of Rutland, I would say that I appreciate the honor you confer on me by the suggestion that I am at this time a proper person to assume the duties of this office. If your suggestion is ratified at the Republican caucus Saturday night, I will be a candidate, and if elected, will do my best to give Rutland a good business administration.*[283]

The theme of debt and financial irresponsibility struck a responsive chord in the public. One letter to the *Herald* stated, "Yes truly, the city of Rutland is 'struggling in the embrace of the whirlpool of needless extravagance' and it is about time that the taxpayer began to realize the importance of electing men to manage our city finances who will pledge themselves to put a stop to it."[284]

Shortly after the Republicans had their caucus, the Democrats met on February 18. Mayor Browne addressed the caucus and urged that no nominee be submitted as mayor. Browne recounted how the Republicans had obstructed his programs and the Democratic aldermen in trying "to manage the city's affairs and suggested the Democratic party would be wise to let the republican nominee for mayoralty be elected and see the republican party try its hand in running the government."

Control of Rutland shifted back and forth in the next decade among Republicans, Democrats and Labor. Mayor in 1899, William Y.W. Ripley (1832–1905) was part of the Civil War generation, a lieutenant colonel in the war and major general of the Home Guard and had come from an old, elite marble family. Ripley had been president of Ripley Sons Marble Company in Center Rutland, later acquired by the Vermont Marble Company. Like the Clements and many of the old marble family elites, he moved into banking, succeeding his father as president of Rutland County National Bank.[285]

CHAPTER 8

TWENTIETH-CENTURY STRUGGLE

Progressivism, a loose collection of reform ideas, appealed to marble elites and workers alike. With its appeal to greater "efficiency," the Progressive movement had an aura of science and education. Because Progressivism encompassed many points of view and objectives, it could gather under its aegis diversified groups that agreed that society must move forward but differed significantly in their visions. Businessmen such as the Proctors saw economic monopoly, to their minds a type of private regulation, as the best way to develop their businesses. The potentially greater political efficiency of the new city government appealed to the financial community headed by the Clements and the Dorrs. For the workers, social democracy, participation in government, would provide a counterbalance to remedy social ills. Charity movements, the Social Gospel movement, the Good Government movement and the Social Settlement movement had their counterparts throughout the Marble Valley. The relatively newly empowered vision of city government in Rutland became a battleground between these competing progressive visions.

Denied power politically, Labor sought to bring about change in a series of strikes. Labor unrest affected Rutland in 1902 and 1904. In 1902, a series of five strikes swept through some of the largest companies in the area. Democrats regained the mayor's office when voters elected David Wells Temple (1854–1930). Temple had settled in Rutland a short time before, in 1897. Along with his brother, J.C. Temple, he founded the Temple Brothers Marble Company. But unlike the traditional marble princes, he was a staunch Democrat and more sympathetic to workers.[286]

In 1902, the political rivalry in the Marble Valley expanded into a statewide conflict. Since workers had no strong party at the state level, they would have to choose from establishment candidates who came closest to their own objectives. The rivalry that had existed at the local level between the Proctors and the Clements now reached the state level. Fletcher Proctor had been road commissioner for ten years and a school board member for twenty. He was a selectman of Rutland in 1884 and 1885 (before the town of Proctor split away). The town of Proctor elected Fletcher to the legislature in 1890, 1900 and 1904; once he received all but one of the votes (the other two times, the vote was unanimous).[287] In 1902, both Fletcher Proctor and P.W. Clement set their sights on the Republican nomination for governor.

P.W. Clement tried to assume the role of political reformer and progressive— friend of the workingman and steadfast opponent of the political machine of the Proctors. Despite his claim to support the worker and his backing of the immigrant issue of "local option" for the sale of alcoholic beverages, Clement's persona of reformer did not ring completely true. In reality, he was a reactionary conservative. When he was finally elected governor, sixteen years later at the 1920 national governors' conference in Harrisburg, Pennsylvania, he distributed a political tract that he had written and published, entitled "Dangers of Centralization in Governmental Functions." It attacked the Sixteenth, Eighteenth and Nineteenth Amendments to the Constitution. According to his pamphlet, income tax, liquor prohibition and women's suffrage had passed only because of special interest groups.[288]

In 1902, in his first bid for governor, Clement focused on "local option," the policy of enabling each political district to decide whether alcohol sales and consumption were permitted or not, a stance favored by many immigrants. Besides promoting the local option on practical grounds, he argued that the prohibition law was an abuse of government power in the name of morality, greed by officers, hypocrisy by citizens and government abuse by the legal system. The disparity between the statewide prohibition law and the lack of observance of the law divided Clement from the Proctors. Clement wanted more transparency and consistency. The Proctors favored more strict observance and followed a policy of dismissing workers who came to work drunk. Clement controlled the local media in Rutland. His *Rutland Daily Herald* covered his campaign speeches thoroughly while paying scant attention to the other two candidates in the Republican primary race: Proctor and McCullough. In an open letter about the Prohibitory Act written

Twentieth-century Struggle

Right: Redfield Proctor (1831–1908) in his later years as a Republican U.S. senator from Vermont. He was many things: colonel in the Union army during the Civil War; member of Vermont state House of Representatives (1867–68, 1888); member of Vermont state Senate (1874–76); lieutenant governor of Vermont (1876–78); governor of Vermont (1878–80); U.S. secretary of war (1889–91); and U.S. senator from Vermont (1891–1908). He died in office in Washington, D.C., on March 4, 1908. *Courtesy of Rutland Historical Society.*

Below: The Proctor family mausoleum in Proctor. Redfield and many members of the Proctor family are buried in the Proctor Cemetery. The mausoleum is in a classic marble style. *Mike Austin Collection.*

in 1902, Clement stated his position on alcohol. It was also an appeal to Republicans and others who were opposed to the strictures of temperance.

Conservative on the issue of alcohol use, and taking the high moral ground, the Proctors represented the more acceptable rural, Republican and anti-immigrant values of total prohibition. In addition to Clement and Proctor, there was a third candidate for the Republican nomination: John G. McCullough, a railroad tycoon from North Bennington. At the state Republican convention, after the second ballot had resulted in none of the three candidates securing a majority, Frank Partridge, who had nominated Proctor, announced that his candidate asked to be withdrawn from consideration, and Partridge gave an additional second to the McCullough nomination, in effect defeating Clement's bid.[289] Denied the Republican nomination by Proctor, in effect giving his votes to McCullough, Clement bolted from the party and decided to challenge what he considered machine politics. The Clement alliance saw the opposition as a "Republican machine" thwarting the rights of the workers. Clement presented himself as the outsider, although he considered the race primarily between himself and Fletcher Proctor. In the general election, the Vermont Constitution provided that the legislature would determine the winner if none of the candidates achieved a majority; the Republican legislature picked McCullough.[290]

In 1904, labor once again mounted a strong local challenge in Rutland. Labor's strength may have been enhanced by a flurry of organizing activity in 1902 and 1904. In 1904, however, an attempted unionization of the marble workers at the Vermont Marble Company and other marble businesses in the Rutland area raised the specter of revolt and social unrest.

In February 1904, the Republicans, Democrats and Labor Party met at their respective caucuses. Temperance and "local option," the issue that divided the "dry" Republican Proctors from the "wet" Percival W. Clement, allowed the Labor Party to gain a foothold with an appeal to the workers and immigrants. The split fragmented the Republican Party, and the Democrats were in disarray. The *Rutland Daily Herald* commented on the orderliness of the Republican and Labor caucuses in contrast to the Democratic caucus. As their candidate for mayor, the Labor Party selected John Carder, and the Republicans, Henry W. Spafford.

With the two major parties divided over issues and candidates, a unified Labor Party triumphed, as the Workingmen had done in 1886 when Rutland was still a village. Carder, a former Knight of Labor and an immigrant from Cornwall, England, secured enough votes to be elected Rutland's first mayor from the Labor Party. The worker victory was, however, short-lived. Carder served from March 1904 to March 1905 before a resurgence of the Republican elites often associated with the marble industry elected J. Forrest Manning, a marble owner, in 1905.

The International Marble Workers' Association of the United States and Canada presented a union contract, dated July 1, to Vermont Marble Company, the Columbian Marble Company and the Florence-Rutland Marble Company; its provisions included a nine-hour workday from 7:00 a.m. to 5:00 p.m. with a one-hour lunch break, double-time for extra hours, elimination of contract work, daily wages set for a number of marble occupations, weekly paychecks and standardized apprenticeships. The local daily worried that a threatened strike would disrupt the local economy, "stop[ping] short the monthly pay roll of about $140,000 as well as disbursements for $100,000 a month extra for coal, lumber and other supplies."[291]

On the evening of July 11, National Union president John A. Fitzgerald, who had presented the contract to local marble company owners on June 20, accused Vermont Marble and the Proctor family of abusing the people of Vermont, saying:

> *Think of his* [Redfield Proctor Sr.] *going down to Cuba and submitting a report on conditions there that brought on a war, while back in Vermont, he knew he had a plantation of white slaves that were in even a worse condition than the Cubans. That he personally conducted a system of slavery far more deplorable than that on the Spanish island, since the subjects were intelligent white people, born and reared to a better lot.*

Fitzgerald threatened to shut down projects around the country that were using Vermont marble, saying that he had a list of sixty-seven work sites that would halt work upon receiving his telegram. The marble workers voted to strike and also to ask the International Association of Machinists to withdraw labor from all the affected mills and quarries.[292] The morning of July 12, workers went to their jobs at 7:00 a.m., picked up their tools and left at 9:00 a.m. The next morning's *Rutland Daily Herald* reported that Columbian Marble Quarrying Company, Temple Brothers and W.R. Kinsman were all shut down and that "the Rutland-Florence company's mills at West Rutland

Vermont Marble Company's sales staff assembled in front of the Proctor YMCA, built for the community by the VMC. *Courtesy of Vermont Marble Museum.*

and Fowler [were] seriously crippled." Vermont Marble Company's finishing departments at West and Center Rutland were "materially affected," and the Proctor plant was also affected "in a measure."[293]

Newspapers across the state took sides as to whether the strike was ultimately "fair" or not. The *Saint Albans Messenger* noted no; marble workers received adequate wages and also benefited from the generosity of the Proctors, providing YMCA, churches and libraries. The *Barre Telegram* sided with the union, noting that civic improvement moneys should have been put instead into worker paychecks so individuals could spend the money their labor generated as they wished.[294] H.L. Hindley in the *Brattleboro Reformer* accepted that paternalism had advantages but felt that they were outweighed by the workers' lack of individual power, saying:

> [T]he fact remains that the Vermont Marble company is running on full time today with practically every other marble firm, run on the "modern plan," tied up dead.
>
> Paternalism is a bad thing, but a successful paternal has more absolute power than the amiable czar of all the Russias.[295]

Over time, the strikers became increasingly restless. Strike wages promised by the union had not yet arrived. Some left the Rutland area looking for work; others found local employment from nearby farmers. In the sixth week of the strike, John V. McCulloch, union secretary-treasurer, moved to Rutland to bolster the strikers' support.[296] The union continued to claim, and Vermont Marble continued to deny, that sympathy with the strikers was slowing work across the United States.[297]

The *Herald*'s columns included a copy of a circular that Vermont Marble had printed, stating its position toward employees and strikers. The company employed about 2,500 men, both union and nonunion. The largest number that went on strike was 325, or about 7 percent of the workforce. The company had turned none of them or their families out of company-owned housing, including the families of men who had left town to find work elsewhere. Nearly half of the initial strikers had returned to work. Advantages of working for Vermont Marble included a low rent for company housing (an average of $5.07 per month compared to an average daily wage of $4.00), company-provided medical and death insurance, free hospital care and low prices at the cooperative company stores. "Less than 3 percent of the entire wages of all our employees was retained by the company for rent, less than 22 percent of it went to these co-operative stores, and over 75 percent was paid in actual cash to our employees."[298]

The company appealed to the workers' sense of place by casting the union organizers as outsiders. The strike, it said, "involved a small number of our employees. It was instigated and is being managed by parties from New York and Chicago." These instigators "have sent out distorted and willfully false reports." The local employees, "either union or non-union," had not filed a complaint against the general conditions or scale of wages, and "our relations were mutually satisfactory." Of the 175 who went out on strike, 110 were Italian stonecutters. According to the company, if the stonecutters disobeyed the orders of the union, "they will be blacklisted and soon will not be permitted to work at their trade as stone cutters, either for us or any one else," and they would be "blacklisted in Italy" as well.[299] Shortly thereafter, the strike collapsed. Striker numbers had dwindled. The old strike committee had been discharged and a new one appointed because strikers were dissatisfied with progress. The union-paid striker wages were not what the men had been led to believe. On September 18, the strikers voted to return to work, 59 to 33, with about 100 abstaining. This was the last significant labor organizing effort in the valley until the 1930s.

The informal mountain rule was that governors should alternate from the east and the west sides of the mountains. With this tradition, the next opportune time for a candidate from the west to run for governor was in 1906. The political struggle between the Proctors and Clement renewed in 1906, and labor was very much concerned. The strike of 1904 made workers more conscious of the need for a political framework supportive of their efforts. Clement's anti-Labor position was known ever since he had strongly opposed Thomas Browne as mayor of Rutland in 1896 and replaced him as mayor in 1897. Could Clement be trusted with the labor vote now if they supported him for governor? To determine his position, the Vermont Federation of Labor sent him a questionnaire. His responses showed that he was not a progressive on labor issues. Labor was concerned about workers being paid on a weekly basis. Clement's response was, "I am not inclined to favor laws of this character which undertake to interpose the hands of the government to settle matters of private interest. I regret the tendency of legislation toward paternalism."[300]

On the issue of an eight-hour day for public government employees, Clement was opposed to any legislation. The federal government a generation earlier had set a standard of an eight-hour workday. Clement stated his opposition:

> *Why give employees an eight-hour day? Neither you nor I are limited by law in our labor to eight hours. The employees of this state are not overburdened in regard to the hours of labor and it would be unwise at this time when we are trying to rescue expenses of state government to needlessly increase them in this way. If elected governor, my influence would be to have the employees of the state give such proper services as the employees of other business do.*[301]

Again and again, Clement rejected Labor's key positions.

Despite Clement's efforts, once more he was shunted aside from the Republican nomination for governor. The Proctor forces controlled the Republican machinery in the state; the nominee of the Republican establishment was Fletcher Proctor. On May 24, 1906, seeing that he was blocked by the Proctor interests from securing nomination, Clement accepted an invitation from a group of citizens to run for governor as an Independent again. Once again, he raised the populist issue of access to alcohol and recounted how the legislature failed to pass a local option law, but in his letter of acceptance as an Independent he also raised another issue of progressives—more representative democracy. Writing from Rutland though not mentioning Proctor by name, he denounced the political and economic power of the "Ring Master" to direct national, state and local interests against the will of the people and for private gain.

In a speech at Bennington on July 28, 1906, he told the crowd:

> *Vermont's political boss is Senator Redfield Proctor. Every man who wants an office in Vermont has to hit the ties for Proctor. The Rutland Railroad has been compelled to take out his sixty pound rails and put in eighty pounds, to accommodate the tremendous travel of office seekers to Proctor. The senator controls the Vermont delegation in Washington and holds federal patronage in his hands; now the son wants to be governor and control State patronage. The old senator holds up one end of the yoke, waves and now and says commandingly: "Haw, Buck; come under." The horns of the independent party are too big and they won't come.*[302]

Clement's appeal fell flat in Rutland County; Proctor won there and in the state. In 1911, Clement represented Rutland in the state legislature. At the same time, he was reelected mayor of Rutland. On June 9, 1912, he resigned his office as mayor when a special election of voters failed to support the mayor's bond issue over a water project. Ironically, Clement and others had used the Moon Brook sewer project to discredit the Democrat and pro-worker Mayor Browne in 1896. Clement submitted a letter of resignation to the city clerk: "Under the circumstances, however, I feel that I can be of no further service in this direction, consequently I hereby resign the office of Mayor of the city of Rutland."[303] In 1918, Clement was finally able to achieve his dream when he won the election for governor. By then, Redfield Proctor Sr. and Fletcher Proctor were both dead, and the election process itself had changed. In 1918, a direct statewide primary replaced town caucuses as the method of selecting the candidates.

Clement and the Proctors were both wealthy, but their legacies for the worker and the valley differed substantially. The Proctors' success, in both business and politics, came from several sources. They felt a strong civic responsibility and related closely to their workers and the valley. The Proctors paid better wages than many companies. The Vermont Marble Company was the largest marble company and despite its monopoly seemed to be concerned with its workers.

In the first and second generation of Proctors, an implied social contract existed between the company and the workers that fostered corporate loyalty and identity. The company improved the overall quality of life for the worker with accident and death insurance and medical support and, in the broader community, support of churches, libraries, health centers, community centers and education. Many remember Fletcher Proctor's interaction with his workers. Ada Stewart, for instance, recalled that Fletcher Proctor "had a remarkable gift of memory for names. The writer thinks he knew the names of everyone of the more than three hundred schoolchildren of Proctor Village, where they lived, and where their fathers worked."[304] The Proctors were very much involved in the social community.

Fletcher Proctor, the successor to Redfield Proctor as president of the Vermont Marble Company, continued the paternalistic practices of his father with the establishment of a YMCA, continued company support for libraries and schools in Proctor and West Rutland and an educational program for the wives and children of the workers that taught household skills. Such reforms weakened the need for worker agitation and a public voice.

Marble construction graced many of the banks and other buildings throughout the valley. Marble adorned the public libraries of Rutland, West Rutland and Proctor and the schools in West Rutland and Proctor. The library in Proctor had special significance for the family. Created with a gift of two thousand books from Redfield Proctor when he was still governor, it was housed in company buildings for a number of years.[305] When Arabella Proctor Holden, daughter of Mrs. Emily Proctor and Senator Redfield Proctor, died in 1913, her mother gave money for the construction of the Proctor Free Library on the east bank of the Otter Creek in memory of her daughter. The year before, when their son Fletcher died, Mrs. Emily Proctor provided funds to the town of Proctor to build a marble bridge as a memorial; it connected the east and west sides of the town, spanning the Otter Creek.[306]

The marble bridge at Proctor replaced an earlier structure crossing Otter Creek. It was built as a memorial to Emily Proctor's son at her instigation. What is also interesting is that the bridge became something of a social dividing line: on the east side the more affluent and management lived, and on the west side were the workers. *Courtesy of Vermont Marble Museum.*

Proctor legacies continue to provide operating money to portions of the town budget for both Proctor and West Rutland. The Proctor Hospital served the community from 1896 to 1973, providing medical care at no cost to marble workers and at minimal cost to residents of the town.[307] Churches, service clubs and government offices also benefited from the marble legacy; they had been given land and, often, marble. The company donated land and/or marble to the Union Church, St. Dominic's Church and the fire station in Proctor; St. Stanislaus Church in West Rutland; and the Italian Aid Society in Center Rutland.

The civic example of the earlier Proctors served as a model for their children. Miss Emily Proctor (1869–1948), daughter of Redfield and Emily Proctor, contributed money to the Proctor Library to buy books published in the native languages of the various groups who had immigrated to work for Vermont Marble Company. The family also gave financial support for cancer research at Harvard and to Booker T. Washington and his work at Tuskegee.[308] In 1894, an epidemic of infantile paralysis spread through the valley, infecting 132 young children and causing 16 deaths. When another outbreak occurred in 1914, Miss Emily Proctor gave $25,000 to the Vermont Board of Health for research on the disease. After a state survey found that Pittsford had the most sunlight of any Vermont town, Emily and Redfield Proctor bought Lucius Kendall's farmland in Pittsford for the sanitarium and then sponsored construction of the Vermont Sanatorium for Tuberculosis, in Pittsford, beginning in 1907.[309]

It became a state institution in 1921, a gift from Redfield Proctor Jr. when it was given to the state along with a $200,000 endowment. The TB sanitarium has ceased to exist, but its land was given over for the training site of the Vermont State Police in 1968.[310]

In 1922, Redfield Proctor Jr. and his sister Emily were among the Rutland County philanthropists who built the Caverly Preventorium, west of the sanitarium, as a center to keep children whom doctors felt might become tubercular from developing the disease.[311] The Proctors gave the institution to the Vermont Tuberculosis Association as a memorial to Dr. Charles S. Caverly of Rutland, who had been instrumental in promoting better hygienic practices in the valley.[312] The Prevent, as it was known in the valley, was in existence from 1923 to 1947 and then became the Caverly Health Center from 1947 to 1973, when it closed because of lack of funds.

The younger Emily Proctor was a progressive reformer in the tradition of Jane Addams. Cavendish House in Proctor was her project. Like the settlement houses in large urban areas, it was a site for women to learn contemporary domestic arts in their new environment and for children to learn gardening and other life skills. As more and more diversified immigrant groups came into the valley, Cavendish House also became a place to come together to learn skills and the English language.[313] It grew from two rooms in the post office building to a separate building of its own.

Like the settlement houses that inspired it, its original purpose was to teach adults and schoolchildren to cook healthier meals with inexpensive foods. Courses in household skills such as knitting, household accounting, history and geography of foods and recipes (what countries they came from), hygiene and, during World War I, in surgical dressing and typewriting were offered. Besides cooking and sewing lessons, Cavendish House offered

English lessons to foreign women. On Monday evenings, Polish and Finnish women met; on Tuesday evenings, Hungarian and Slavic women met. During the summer months, gardening skills were taught, and summer school classes were held for students who did not pass in the public school. Cavendish House provided bath and shampoo rooms free to women and children. Children who came from a distance were served hot lunches with milk at a minimum cost.[314]

In an age of Frederick Taylor's scientific management, with its emphasis on the amount of time to produce the product, the previous corporate concern for the worker and the worker's community—so evidenced by the first and second generations of Proctors—increasingly shifted from its earlier paternalism to an emphasis on economic and managerial control of the worker. Simultaneously, the economic power of marble, which supported the political power, also began to weaken. At the beginning of the 1920s, marble was still the most quarried and valued stone, but granite production was increasing in quantity and value.[315] By the end of the 1920s, granite had surpassed marble in value and production in Vermont.[316] By the time President Roosevelt visited Barre in 1936, that city had become the center of granite production in America.

By the 1930s, marble workers in the Marble Valley, nearly all employed by the Vermont Marble Company, received far lower wages than the granite workers in eighty separate granite companies.[317]

Marble workers complained of excessive deductions from their pay for rent, electricity, water, insurance, hospitalization and even cow pasturage. Marble polishers were forced to buy the polishing heads for the company's machines and pay for the polishing powder. Men received weekly paychecks of two cents, twenty cents or sixty-eight cents. When the Depression hit, many received pink vouchers marked "No Check" in ink; others were in debt for rent on company-owned houses because they were working only a few hours a week. Towns were filled with unemployed marble workers ready to take jobs if the employed men became dissatisfied.

In the winter and spring of 1935–36, the Danby, West Rutland and Proctor employees of the company staged one of the most bitter strikes Vermont had ever witnessed. On November 2, in an act of solidarity, the marble workers of Rutland Local 94 of the Industrial Association of Marble Workers met at the Moose Hall on Center Street and decided to support the

Danby workers. The action, however, was a cautious sign of support and unity for the Danby quarrymen and not an official action of the Rutland Local 94 union. Instead of striking, on November 4, 1935, the men voted to go on "holiday."

The company claimed that it could not meet the demands of the workers because it had been working at a loss for several years.[318] The holiday-takers, not trusting this statement, took forceful action. They stopped trucks at the West Rutland lime plant and nonunion members' trucks were stoned as they went through the picket lines.[319] By the third day of the "holiday," the West Rutland, Danby and Center Rutland Mills had closed. Only the Proctor plant, site of the company headquarters, remained open.[320] Eugene Pederson, head of the West Rutland union, held a meeting to ask the members to sanction a strike. His plea was translated into Italian and Polish for the non-English speakers. The company responded by securing eighty-five deputies and sheriffs from four different counties. During the course of the nine-month struggle, the salaries of sixty-five state and town deputies were openly paid by the Vermont Marble Company.[321]

The Rutland County Communist Party then urged the workers at Proctor to join with the other holiday-takers. Members of the Communist Party of Rutland City distributed leaflets in West Rutland door to door that read in part:

> *Proctor is working! Strike Proctor! Pickett Proctor!...The Communist Party of Rutland City congratulates you for your militant action. Keep up the good work. The communist members in your locals are fighting to win this strike and to make these unions strong.*[322]

By the sixth day, the holiday had become an official strike.[323] Small brawls broke out.[324] On November 22, 1935, one thousand men marched through West Rutland in support of the strike.[325] After the company cut rents on housing to those who did not strike, strikers stoned the houses in West Rutland and Center Rutland; deputies had to escort workers through the picket lines.[326]

On January 6, 1936, the company attempted to run in scab labor, and the striking workmen joined the battle. At one time during that day, seventy figures lay in the bloody snow.[327] It was a winter of the severest privation.

In the winter and spring of 1935–36, the Danby, West Rutland and Proctor employees of the company went out on one of the most bitter strikes Vermont had ever witnessed. The strike divided the workers and management. In this picture, notice how one participant, Roy Spear, is carrying a machine gun. Some workers carried axes to protect themselves. *Courtesy of Rutland Historical Society.*

Weekly contributions to a strike relief fund were made by fellow union workers in Barre, Graniteville and Websterville and by many educational and social institutions. Some officials sided with the company. John Dwyer, for instance, a selectman and one of the town overseers of the poor, was also a foreman for the Vermont Marble Company. He was convicted in court of withholding town aid for destitute schoolchildren.[328]

Company housing was also used by both sides. The company sent letters to 186 strikers who lived in company housing informing them that they must vacate by April 1. These workers had not paid any rent, electric or water bills since the beginning of the strike.[329] On February 24, five marble strikers—Hilford Johnson, John DeSaint, Zignment Kantorski, Steve Czachor and Paul Yascot—attacked Carl Peterson, a nonstriking marble worker, hospitalizing him. The strikers punched him and used pipes, bottles and stones when Peterson was walking home from work. The five strikers were later convicted and sent to the state prison in Windsor for one to two years. This incident was the only trial of the strike.[330]

As the conflict escalated, the company deputized the largest police force in Vermont's history.[331] In March, the company agreed to an independent auditor to justify its position that it did not have enough money to pay the workers. In April, radical strikers dynamited power lines leading to the Danby Quarry, and a power plant at West Rutland was torched.[332] Given the severe financial plight of many of the citizens, the state attorney general's office authorized a $500 reward for information leading to the capture and conviction of those responsible.[333]

Around the Memorial Day holiday, Rockwell Kent, the well-known socialist and writer, held public hearings in West Rutland to advocate the workers' situation. The company claimed that it was broke, yet it paid a 15 percent dividend to shareholders in 1935. The state paid for sixteen sheriffs and deputies but gave no state aid to the strikers. According to testimony, the company stirred up ethnic rivalry by favoring ethnic groups it considered more docile.[334] Several people testified before an inquiring committee about the impact on families. One mother testified that her milk allocation was cut from two quarts a day to one quart, adding more pressure to care for her six children. She was told by the overseer of the poor, who also was a manager in the Vermont Marble Company, "You can keep the children quiet on water." To another mother who stated that she had but one pair of underclothes per child during that bitter winter, the overseer stated, "Put them to bed when you wash their underclothes."[335]

Strikers received sympathetic support from higher education institutions such as nearby Dartmouth College and Bennington College and farther away from Skidmore College and the University of Wisconsin.[336] The student newspaper at Dartmouth, where Redfield Proctor Sr. had gone to school, took up collections of food and clothing. Nobel Prize winner Sinclair "Red" Lewis, who took part in the strike, recalled that the local police forces, influenced by the economic and political power of the Vermont Marble Company and the Proctors, did not allow the donations to reach the workers.[337]

At the beginning of July, the company shut off electricity, generated by the company at the Falls, to fifty-seven houses, although it had continued to supply electricity to the homes since the November strike began. The company also evicted six families for nonpayment.[338] The bitter strike ended on July 26, 1936, when 86 percent of 350 strikers agreed to go back to work. The Vermont Marble Company had held its ground against the strikers, although for workers who were still working it maintained a two-and-a-half-cent pay raise that had started in April. The agreement provided that workers in company housing could stay as long as they paid current rent and arranged to pay utilities and back rent within one year.[339] The company took men back when it needed them, but at the same time it did not lay off any of the replacement workers. Hard feelings between these groups would fester for some time.

This was a period of bitter labor conflict nationwide. In 1937, there were 4,720 strikes, and 2,728 of them were over labor's right to organize. In response to the sit-down strikes in the automobile industry at Flint, Michigan, and Akron, Ohio, Vermont representative Ernest Dunklee introduced legislation making sit-down strikes illegal, and the General Assembly of 1937 passed it.[340]

The *Rutland Herald* looked back on the strike as the result of the end of "kindly feudalism." The mutual respect and dependence between company and worker had broken down. Frank Partridge and other associates, who came from a corporate rather than paternalistic perspective, were more inflexible than earlier managers and, perhaps forced by the economic times, took the hard line with the strikers. In the midst of the tumultuous strike, he semiretired in 1935 but continued to serve as board chair.[341] Partridge's positions enraged the workers, helping to set off the prolonged strike. Redfield Proctor Jr., fifty-six years old, was vice-president of the company in 1935 and inheritor of the Proctor mantle.[342] Perhaps if Redfield Proctor had exerted more authority, the strike would not have lasted so long or have been so bitter. The pattern of behavior in the marble strike was very similar to that of the steel strike in Homestead over a generation earlier, when Henry Clay Frick took the hard line against the workers while owner Andrew Carnegie removed himself from the scene.[343]

The hope of the workers after the strike was to return to work and help shape the public dialogue with legislation. But the worker voice never captured the resilient hope of 1886 when James Hogan and the fifteen Workingmen justices were voted into office or of 1896 when Thomas Browne had won the office of mayor with workers support or in 1904 when John S. Carder, Rutland's only Labor mayor, triumphed over a divided Democrat and Republican opposition.

The Workingmen's democracy had fallen victim to corporate power. The economic and political threat in the United States and of the worker and had been contained, but one unfortunate cost of that containment was the suppression of labor's voice in the public and political dialogue. For labor, it was an exorbitant price to pay. The citizen-worker was reluctant to run for office. Even today, despite the fact that Rutland County is essentially a working-class community, its county representatives often have corporate rather than worker thinking. At the local level there is no Labor Party. In the late twentieth century, the Progressive Party of Vermont emerged to carry on the traditions and keep the voice of the citizen-worker alive as part of the civil dialogue.[344] Vermont's three-member U.S. Congressional delegation currently has one Independent and two Democrats. Once more, the social democracy issues of the Progressives are part of the public dialogue affecting the citizen-worker in Vermont.

CONCLUSION

Legacies

Along with colonial land speculators, subsistence farmers rushed in to acquire the last major undeveloped land in the corner of New England. The valley achieved its first measure of significant financial success as sheep farming progressed from a subsistence level to an industry of national significance from 1810 to the 1850s, and for a time wheat farming became important as well. But the hardscrabble Vermont farmland, at first a breadbasket, succumbed to the more fertile farmlands of the Midwest, and the newly constructed Erie Canal allowed for relatively easy transport of farm goods and other material to the East. So Vermont needed to find another basis for its economy—one that could not easily be dislodged.

It was marble that transformed the valley and left a more lasting legacy. Early entrepreneurs, such as William F. Barnes, proved that marble could return dramatic profits. The next generation of entrepreneurs expanded the industry, and the scale grew with the arrival of Redfield Proctor in 1869. Proctor learned management and human resource skills in the Civil War and perfected them in Vermont's marble industry. He unified small, disparate marble companies, forming cartels and using his positions in government to aid his enterprise.

Under the management of Redfield Proctor and the Proctor family, the marble industry brought about dramatic change to the valley, improvements that still bear their civic imprint today. Redfield Proctor emphasized and promoted a traditional moral code, both for himself and his workers. He supported libraries and churches. His son hired the first industrial nurse and

The Proctor family. Emily Proctor, wife of Redfield Proctor, is on the extreme right. This was a remarkable family, involved in philanthropic, educational, health, business and political concerns in the region. Redfield Proctor achieved success on the national level as secretary of war and U.S. senator from Vermont. *Courtesy of Rutland Historical Society.*

supported a local hospital. The Proctor family founded the first industrial YMCA in the state (and possibly in the country). Later, as the Proctor family grew concerned that core moral values were more important than the sectarianism that a YMCA might promote, the local YMCA became the nondenominational Sutherland Club, open to all male employees of the company. Eventually the club admitted women and junior and senior high students. It provided a social setting for community meetings.[345]

Many workers, both foreign and U.S.-born, made their first real estate investment with Proctor's help. He allowed them to purchase company-built houses or company-owned land on which to build their homes. He subsidized scholarships for young men to go to college; a fund set up by the Proctor family still continues to provide college scholarships to Proctor High School graduates. The electric generating plant at Proctor, built about 1905 at the instigation of Fletcher Proctor, provided electricity not only for the marble company's quarries and mills but also for the houses of Proctor residents.[346]

The Vermont Marble Company radiated influence throughout the valley. Studies of the marble industry have often focused only on those directly involved in working the white metamorphic rock, overlooking the subsidiary organizations that developed to support the industry. Vermont Marble, at least initially, owned many of these support organizations. For example, before the marble industry became mechanized, the company-owned farms operated to supply food for the draft animals (horses and oxen) that pulled the marble on "stone boats" or wagons from quarry edge to mill and from mill to railroad.

The company also acquired land around Proctor Pond and employed an entirely separate workforce to cut, transport and shape the timber needed to box and ship the marble. The timber, worked at Vermont Marble sawmills, was used for the construction of derricks, company structures, worker housing, fuel and possibly even railroad ties when the company constructed its own Clarendon & Pittsford Railroad, utilizing its own engineers and crews to lay the track and its own railroad workers to operate the enterprise. Built to transport marble from the finishing mills to distribution points, the railroad also functioned as a "milk run," carrying supplies, food and workers.

The labor of the citizen-worker added to civic architecture in the valley and across the nation. The legacy of Vermont Marble is part of nearly every vista in central Vermont. In nearly every downtown, marble appears as a component of many buildings' basic structure—as steps, pillars, sills and lintels and also as walkways and curbs. Crushed marble forms the hidden drainage underlayment of parking lots and green spaces. The company donated land and/or marble for churches, schools, libraries and community services like the firehouse and cemeteries in Proctor and the Italian Aid Society in Center Rutland. The company was often involved in civic projects. Marble from central Vermont quarries graces personal, state and national civic architecture and monuments, including headstones at Arlington National Cemetery, the Tomb of the Unknown Soldier in Washington, D.C., the Indiana Statehouse in Indianapolis, the Washington State Capitol, the U.S. Supreme Court building, the Thomas Jefferson Memorial and the United Nations building in New York City.

Over thirty years, from 1870 to 1900, the marble worker gained in substantial ways. Workers had company healthcare and wages had risen; the company store was more a convenience for the workers than, as it had been earlier, an effort to recapture their paychecks. While many workers were well satisfied with conditions in the company, others were not, and all workers wanted their voices to count. From 1886, when the division of

Those who fought for the Union in the American Civil War were eligible to join the Grand Army of the Republic. Its headquarters on West Street in Rutland were razed to erect today's Rutland Post Office and federal offices. *Courtesy of Rutland Historical Society.*

Rutland took place, to the early twentieth century, workers challenged and helped to shape the public dialogue. Their physical labor had contributed, literally, to carving out the economy of the valley, just as labor leaders such as James Hogan, Thomas Browne and John Carder carved out a vision of a better life for workers in the Marble Valley. The Knights of Labor organized workers to define this vision according to its social and economic agenda.

Workers moved increasingly into the public forum, fashioning a sense of political place, in an attempt to safeguard their workplace.[317] Politics provided a legal framework of worker compassion and concerns. The citizen-worker continued to rise to the civic responsibility of leadership. One example was Jack Carder, a Welsh marble worker, who was elected as mayor of Rutland City on the Labor ticket in 1904.

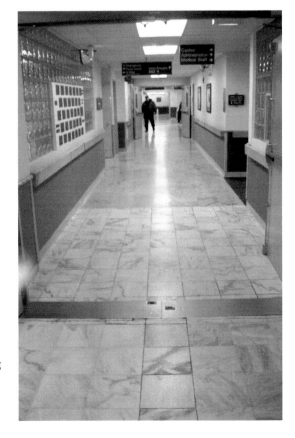

Above: The West Rutland Library is essentially two large rooms plus a basement. The Proctor family donated books for its establishment. *Mike Austin Collection.*

Right: A Rutland Regional Medical Center hallway, an example of contemporary use of the marble in floors of various area structures. Vermont marble has been used for the Supreme Court building and in many places throughout the country to suggest beauty and gracefulness. *Mike Austin Collection.*

However, there was a downside to the struggle for power. The division of Rutland into separate towns showed the underside of distrust. Although Rutland experienced an east-west religious geographic tension from its early foundation, by the nineteenth century that tension had exploded along economic and social lines. Rutland had, for a time, overtaken its economic rival, Burlington, as the largest city in the state, but in the struggle for power in the 1880s Rutland imploded, divided along the economic planes of city and countryside in disputes between the village and periphery. The legacy of that split hampers development today, especially in Rutland City.

After 1900, the deterioration of company-worker relationships began. The Vermont Marble Company had a constant oversupply of workers about the turn of the century. Thus the issue was not so much the conditions at the quarries and the mills as the opportunity to work for the major employer in the area.

In the first two decades of the twentieth century, the workers seemed to have made progress; after 1904, there was no significant labor conflict. However, the workers unintentionally muted their own voices by misjudging management. When Redfield Proctor managed the Vermont Marble Company, he lived and worked close to his workers. Later, as management increasingly removed itself from the workers' daily social lives, a combination of influences and forces gradually disempowered the worker.

By the 1930s, economic forces outside and inside the valley had shifted the management philosophy so much that it no longer valued the ideal of a close, tightly knit community with civic responsibility. The relationship between worker and company degenerated into bitterness and distrust. For two generations, the bloody strike of 1934–35 stood out as a haunting memory of the marble industry's decline.[348] Much that workers and management had fostered, such as insurance, healthcare and civic projects, as well as intangible qualities such as concern and social recognition for the workers, now seemed relegated to an earlier time.

The marble worker, however, had carved out an enduring sense of place that still benefits the people of the valley. Though the workers' voices were muted from the 1930s onward, the significant contributions of that earlier generation of managers and workers remain with us today. Like other laborers of the time, the marble workers educated themselves on public issues and entered into the political process. Their voices soon dwindled, however. Woodrow Wilson, observing a change taking place in his lifetime, and accelerating in ours, commented, "As a nation we are becoming civically illiterate. Unless we find better ways to educate ourselves as citizens, we run the risk of drifting unwittingly into a new kind of Dark Age—a time when small cadres of specialists will control knowledge and thus control the decision making process."[349]

Vermont at one time had over 700 working quarries; approximately 180 remain in operation today.[350] The Vermont Marble Company and its quarries have been carved up. In 1978, marble dealer Stanley Gawett bought all the Vermont Marble Company property in West Rutland.[351] Only a few small marble companies—Gawett Marble and Granite, Proctor Marble Company, Vermont Quarries Corporation and the largest and inheritor of the Vermont Marble Company, OMYA—remained, shadows of what once had been. OMYA, an international company specializing in calcium carbonate products, acquired the Vermont Marble Company and still works some of the quarries.[352]

Marble is still quite valuable and scarce. There are more gold mines in the United States than there are marble quarries. However, OMYA has been forced to find new markets for marble in face of competition from synthetic building products. The company has transformed the marble business from a construction stone company to a world supplier of calcium carbonate and marble slurry (used in toothpaste, paper, paint, detergents, electrical components and many other products).

The marble workers sought a wider participatory democracy that enfranchised not just the elite but all the worker-citizens of the valley. The marble they worked so hard to extract and finish has become an ironic symbol of their struggle. Marble, once the symbol of wealth and decoration for a small elite, now supports the everyday needs of many in the form of calcium carbonate in toothpaste and other essential personal and cleaning products.

OMYA continues in the legacy of civic responsibility laid down by the three generations of Proctors. In recent years, OMYA has shown its concern with planned reclamation of land and financial support for the community and community projects. In fiscal year 2001, OMYA contributed to seventy-one Rutland County organizations, such as private and public schools and humanities projects—examples include Cross Roads Arts Council and the Paramount Theatre, public television and service clubs such as Brownies and Girl Scouts and health organizations.[353] Today, OMYA employs approximately eight hundred workers, one-third of the number of workers at Vermont Marble Company in the early 1900s.

The political power of the region as a whole, and of the Vermont Marble Company in particular, has declined. Marble industry corporations influenced Vermont until the early 1960s. In the first half of the twentieth century, most Vermont governors had connections directly and indirectly with the marble industry, and many came from Marble Valley. Redfield Proctor, two of his sons and one grandson were governors of Vermont. Of the seven presidents of the Vermont Marble Company during its existence, five also served as governors of the state, and one was a U.S. senator. After 1960, political power shifted, and Rutland's rival, Burlington in Chittenden County, became the state's power base. Control of the Vermont Marble Company itself moved outside the valley, even outside the country. OMYA is headquartered in Switzerland. The Vermont Quarries Corporation, a subsidiary of a joint Italian partnership known as R.E.D., runs the Danby Quarry, previously owned by the Vermont Marble Company since 1902 and once one of the largest underground marble quarries in the world. Officially, the Vermont Marble Company went out of business in 1992.[354]

The railroads, which had helped to make Rutland so important in the late nineteenth and early twentieth centuries, started their economic and strategic decline in the middle of the twentieth century. Transportation, which was so central to Rutland's development in the nineteenth century, now impeded it. A modern interstate highway connection between Rutland and Burlington and on to Montreal, following the earlier railroad systems, was thwarted by Massachusetts, which wanted an interstate connecting to one of its major cities, Springfield, in the western part of that state. The interstate system was instead built both west and east of Rutland, leaving the city stranded with its outdated transportation system. Development of an international airport in Burlington further isolated Rutland. The geography of the mountains and the valleys, which had made railroad construction difficult but possible for Rutland, now proved a significant barrier for a major airport. Rutland developed a small commuter airport that struggled against the larger economy of the north.

In the past, Rutland was able to shift from one economic base to another to help it remain in the forefront of the state's economy. No new vision, economic base or entrepreneur has emerged to move Rutland to a new prosperity. In the late twentieth and early twenty-first centuries, no engine of growth appeared comparable to those in its early history. The most dynamic and extensive of these engines, and the one that had given the region its greatest influence locally and nationally, was the marble industry. The region's own sense of identity came from the marble influence and the rich deposits of marble. The fragmentation of Rutland into separate towns, looked upon as a favorable move in the nineteenth century, now retarded growth in the twentieth and the twenty-first centuries. Instead of cooperation in the region, the divided towns competed with one another for increasingly scarce resources. The bitterness of the 1935–36 strike divided West Rutland and Proctor, making West Rutland the butt of many jokes, especially anti-Polish jokes.

Local mythology tends to show Vermont Marble Company in a poor light, spreading the 1930s-era turmoil over the entire lifespan of the firm. A significant portion of that character blackening can probably also be traced to the longevity of P.W. Clement's earlier influence on the *Rutland Herald*, which negatively colored any mention of the Proctor family.

The first and second generation of Proctors, more so than the other elites of the time, helped to transform the valley with a sense of corporate and civic responsibility. P.W. Clement, for instance, despite all of his wealth and influence, did not contribute civically in the way that families such as the Proctors (or, for that matter, the Dorrs) did. Workers were also involved in this public, private and civic dialogue. The initial board of the Proctor Hospital had top management, middle management, office workers and members of the community, including women, on the board. Unlike in the 1850s and 1860s, the later generation of workers, up until the 1920s, identified with the company even as workers sought their own political voices.

The focus of this book has been to examine the essential context of place so that visitors and citizens of the area can develop a much better understanding of—and appreciation for—the region and its people. In order to understand the Marble Valley, one must understand the marble workers who shaped the region. I have sought to draw them into the narrative to demonstrate how the workers, as well as local elites, acted from their own interests and from the sense of place, at times joining forces with others who shared larger common goals. Both class position and a sense of place were important to workers as they tried to influence events.

The political battles over place were fought precisely because the wealth came from particular locales within Rutland. Defensiveness and aggressiveness formed the political argument around place and explain the division of Rutland today. The local elites were themselves divided (urban v. rural) on important issues and conflicts. Their opposition and alliances with the working class helped fuel the complex and fascinating struggle. The very splintering of Rutland into Proctor, West Rutland, Rutland City and the leftover Rutland Town was one result. The workers were the catalyst that galvanized all of the groups into action. To tell the story of the Marble Valley, and specifically of Rutland, without that voice and the struggle of place is to miss an essential part of the story.

Today, the valley awaits another transformation. Unlike the earlier activism of the citizen-worker, who not only voted but also organized and ran for office, the current low participation of the citizenship in national politics shows a dismal sense of alienation and perhaps hopelessness. The earlier model of participatory democracy and corporate responsibility can serve as a guide to renewal. The political voice and the economic contributions of the earlier marble worker helped to shape the valley and form a community in which thousands of citizen-workers lived, worked, voted and sought office as part of their social contract of citizenship. Their choices, like the marble they extracted, shaped and finished, contributed to an exceptional sense of identity and place of which the worker-citizens were justifiably proud despite all of the obstacles. They left a legacy that still continues to benefit the citizens of the Marble Valley.

NOTES

Chapter 1

1. The land between present-day New York and New Hampshire had been a flash point of contention for centuries. The western Abenaki ("People of the Dawn") had used this land for hunting but frequently were in conflict with rival confederations of Iroquois who also used this land for hunting and gathering. When the European invasion took place toward the beginning of the seventeenth century, the tribes sought alliances with the Europeans to further their own objectives. Thus natives and Europeans reinforced the instability of settlement in the area. Rival European powers also challenged one another for possession of the land. The Dutch, the English and the French, at one time or another, claimed the land. When the English ousted the Dutch, the English challenged the French for the land from New York to present-day Maine.

   For nearly a century, the frontier was precarious for any settlement but especially for any settlements near rivers and lakes of the region. Lake Champlain and the Hudson River, and the roads leading to and from them, became keys to a continental power struggle. English and French moved up and down these waterways trying to destroy the other's settlements and fortifications. In so doing, the colonists became familiar with the potential of the land for trading and settlement. With the capitulation of the French in 1759, the English were in no mood for half-way treaties and forced the French from North America (except for two small islands off the Canadian coast and some islands in the Caribbean).

Now northern New England was English, and the dispute was between New Hampshire and New York. Eventually, the settlers entered into the struggle and sought independence from both of those colonies. Now there was land to acquire, and a land rush ensued. For early history of Vermont, see Thompson, *History of Vermont*; Collins, *A History of Vermont*; Montpelier Historical Society, *Essays in the Early History of Vermont*; and La Fayette, *Early History of Vermont*. For more recent scholarship of the general history of Vermont, see Albers, *Hands on the Land*; Doyle, *Vermont Political Tradition*; and Klyza and Trombulak, *Story of Vermont*.

2. MacKenzie, *Indian Ways to Stage Coach Days*, 33.

3. Smith and Rann, eds., *History of Rutland County*, 18.

4. The language of the charter was *pro forma*, portraying Benning Wentworth as the dutiful agent of the king working in the best interests of England and contributing to the national security by setting aside on Pine Hill land for the Royal Navy and also setting aside land for the Church of England. Patriotism and religion were combined, and added to each charter was land set aside for Wentworth from which he could profit. Before the Peace Treaty ending the French and Indian War was signed in Paris in 1760, Benning Wentworth granted 63 townships. On September 7, 1761, Wentworth granted the land known as Rutland and Pittsford. By 1764, Governor Wentworth had granted a total of 131 townships in Vermont and acquired sixty-five thousand acres for himself.

New York also eyed the territory after the recent war. Lieutenant Governor Cadwallader Colden of New York also began to grant patents to the same land. During the year 1765, Colden granted 151 military patents, which covered 131,800 acres. Lord Dunmore—for whom Lake Dunmore in the Brandon area, the northern part of the valley, is named—was appointed royal governor of New York in 1770. Dunmore granted even more land to the same area than did Wentworth and Colden. Between February 28 and July 8, 1770, Dunmore granted 511,900 acres. Dunmore established the town of Socialborough, consisting of 48,000 acres, which was the same area that Wentworth had granted in the Rutland and Pittsford land grant. A third grant of this same territory, known as Fairfield, was issued in 1761 to John Henry Lydius, a fur trader from Albany. The overlapping and conflicting claims led to rivalry between the Hampshire and York claimants. Local enforcers such as the Green Mountain Boys sought to validate the Hampshire grants at the expense of the Yorkers. See *Essays in the Early History of Vermont* and La Fayette, *Early History of Vermont*.

5. Batchellear, *New Hampshire Grants*, 386–89.
6. Swift, *Vermont Place-Names*, 11.
7. See Gilmore, "Connecticut and the Foundation of Vermont." So many settlers came to Vermont from Connecticut that for a time the area was known as New Connecticut.
8. Swift, *Vermont Place-Names*, 61.
9. The area west of New Hampshire and east of New York was prime territory for speculators. Both colonies saw this territory as an extension of their own areas. Because of the vagueness of the charter of New Hampshire and acquired land of New York in a showdown with the Dutch, and then New York's own vague charter, each colony saw the land as a lucrative buffer and desired to grant local charters for land to speculators and settlers from their own regions to solidify their own claims. For background on the early settlement in Rutland, see Petersen, *Otter Creek*, 27.
10. Swan, *Early Families*, 369.
11. Ibid., 410.
12. Boardman also owned part of the cedar swamp that became a site of one of the valley's marble quarries. Swan, *Early Families*, 55.
13. Swan, *Early Families*, 55.
14. James Davidson, interview, October 2009. James Davidson is a local historian and on the board of the Rutland Historical Society. See also Hemenway, *History of Rutland County*, 1017.
15. "First Constitution," *Vermont State Papers*, 244.
16. Perkins's account of his early travel in Vermont was an assessment of what could be done to counter the threat of the "unchurched." Connecticut viewed Vermont as its moral responsibility, since many early settlers were from Connecticut and had family connections to that state, the most famous being the Allen family. Perkins, *A Narrative of Tour*, 15–21.
17. Hemenway, *History of Rutland County*, 1020.
18. See the 1791 Census and the 1800 Census for Rutland County. Over 90 percent of the county residents were of English stock and Protestant. The U.S. First Census, 1791, Population Manuscript for Rutland County. Vermont became the fourteenth state.
19. Dwight, *Travels through the State of North America*, 396.
20. U.S. Third Census, 1810, Population Manuscript for Rutland County.
21. Hemenway, *History of Rutland County*, 1045.
22. Ibid., 1046.
23. Reverend Braislin, "Baptist."
24. Hands, "An Emigrant's Chances," 111–12.
25. Balivet, "Vermont Sheep Industry," 43.

26. At the request of Governor Dillingham, Alonzo B. Valentine—the state commissioner of agriculture and manufacturing interests—traced the beginning of the decline in agriculture in the 1830s and the shift to a new economy in a written report from 1889–90: "As early as 1837 a perceptible diminution of cultivated acres was observed. The year 1840 found the tide of emigration from the State fairly in motion. This was coincidence with the following Great Panic of 1837. Our manufactures of iron and textile fabrics, then in their infancy, were closed, business came to a standstill, and the home market for farm produce was greatly curtailed." See Valentine, *Report of the Commissioner*, 7–8.
27. Petersen, *Otter Creek*, 128.
28. Ambrose I. Brown and Edgar I. Brown attended the meeting from Rutland; in addition to Conant, A.W. Birchard and M.W. Birchard were from Brandon. *Rutland Herald*, September 5, 1835.
29. Petersen, *Otter Creek*, 128.
30. As Yankees moved west, they took with them one of Vermont's contributions to the world. In 1853, descendants of "Figure," the progenitor of the breed that became known as the Morgan horse, won state fair competitions in three different midwestern states: Ohio, Michigan and Indiana. For the attraction of the Midwest for Vermonters, see Wilson, *Hill Country of Northern New England*, 56.
31. *Rutland Herald*, April 21, 1859.
32. Ibid., January 3, 1843.
33. Ibid., August 20, 1843.
34. Petersen, *Otter Creek*, 129.
35. *Rutland Herald*, December 3, 1846.
36. Petersen, *Otter Creek*, 129.
37. Hannon, *Historical Sketches on West Rutland*, 52.
38. Hance, *History of Rutland, Vermont*, 532. $10,000 would be approximately $189,000 in contemporary value. See McCusker, "Comparing the Purchasing Power." $297,000 in 1850 dollars would be approximately $6,290,000 in contemporary evaluation; see Williamson, "What is Relative Value?" Based on Census of Manufacturing 1850. See also Hance, *History of Rutland, Vermont*, 542.
39. Bennett, *Narrative of a Recent Journey*, 25–29.
40. U.S. Census, 1860. Additional, personal communication with Mary Lee Dunn regarding her research for her master's thesis at the University of Massachusetts, July 3, 2002.
41. In a biography about St. George's Catholic Church in northern Vermont, the author noted, "French Catholics traveled back and forth between lower New England and Canada, and even settled in parts of northern Vermont from time to time. Many Catholic Canadians took

refuge in Vermont during Canada's Papineau Rebellion in 1837." See the St. George's webpage at www.uvm.edu.

42. Stillwell, *Migration from Vermont*, 184.
43. Johnson, *Proctor*, 39–40. Also see the St. George's webpage at www.uvm.edu.
44. Hale, "Marble Valley's UN," 37.
45. For the decline of the population and migration from Vermont during these decades, see Stillwell, *Migration from Vermont*, 171–213.
46. U.S. Second Census, 1800, Population Manuscript for Rutland County, and U.S. Seventh Census, 1850, Population Manuscript for Rutland County; U.S. Seventh Census, 1850, Population Manuscript for Chittenden County.

Chapter 2

47. Mango, "Interview on Geographic Formation", February, 4, 2010.
48. To the west of the Marble Valley and extending into New York is the Slate Valley. Vermont slate, as it is often called, is one of the three major slates of the world, the other two being Welch and Spanish slate. Farther north and east, near the capital of the state, is another rich source of minerals. In this area, especially near Barre, are located rich deposits of granite. Of the three major minerals in Vermont, granite was quarried extensively and later than the other two. The immigrants played a significant role in the quarrying industry in Vermont. The Irish were the first immigrant group to work the marble quarries in the Marble Valley; the Welsh, because of their experience at the vast Dinorwig quarry in Wales, brought know-how to the slate quarry industry. In 1850, the first Welsh immigrants arrived in Fair Haven, and in 1852 thirty Welsh settlers arrived in Middle Granville. Several slate companies were formed. The biggest problem early on was the transportation of the quarried stone, such as marble and slate.
49. Humphrey, *Story of Dorset, Vermont*, 71.
50. Smith and Rann, *History of Rutland County*, 179.
51. Hance, *History of Rutland, Vermont*, 526.
52. Ibid.
53. Ibid., 530.
54. Smith and Rann, *History of Rutland County*, 119.
55. William Barnes was the father of William F. Barnes, the most innovative of the middle generation marble entrepreneurs before Redfield Proctor. The father left the area for the westward migration, but William F. Barnes stayed in the area and was the most significant

leader of his generation. See also Hemenway, *History of Rutland County*, 1066.

56. George E. Hall of Cleveland, Ohio, was one of the earliest of the new visionary entrepreneurs. Before considering a purchase of a large tract of marble lands, Hall commissioned Charles H. Hitchcock, a professor and geologist from Dartmouth in Hanover, New Hampshire, to examine the area. Hitchcock's early report comments on the quality of the marble, not only in the valley in general, from Middlebury to Dorset, but especially in the heart of the valley—from Brandon to West Rutland. See also Caverly, *History of the Town of Pittsford*, 521–25.

57. Vermont Bureau of Publicity, *Industrial Vermont*, 19.

58. Hannon, *Biography of St. Bridget's Parish*, 59.

59. *Rutland Herald*, May 16, 1837.

60. Hance, *History of Rutland, Vermont*, 491.

61. Ibid., 534.

62. Gale, *Proctor*, 69. See also *Rutland News*, which published an interview with Daniel Austin in September 1915 about the railroad coming to Proctor in 1849.

63. Hance, *History of Rutland, Vermont*, 525.

64. *Rutland County Independent*, February 17, 1872; *Rutland Herald*, January 9, 22 and 27 and February 23, 1868.

65. The quarry had been originally deeded to Ebenezer Blanchard in October 1794 for the sum of five pounds and was in constant use from 1815 to 1851. For further background, see *Rutland Daily Herald*, January 12, 1881.

66. Hance, *History of Rutland, Vermont*, 528–29.

67. U.S. Seventh Census, 1850, Industrial Manuscript Records.

68. Valentine, *Report of the Commissioner*, 20.

69. Barnes remained in the marble business until May 1871, when he was crushed in one of his quarries by a falling rock; see *Rutland Daily Herald*, May 8, 1871.

70. Hance, *History of Rutland, Vermont*, 532.

71. Hitchcock, Hitchcock Jr., Hager and Hitchcock, *Report on the Geology of Vermont*, 773.

72. Ullery, comp., *Men of Vermont*, 98–99. Before Redfield Proctor, Page was the most politically prominent of the local elites in the 1850s and 1860s. Upon his father William Page's 1849 retirement, John became cashier of the community's oldest bank, the Bank of Rutland. Page was an active proponent for Rutland growth. He was collector and treasurer of the newly formed Rutland Village Corporation in 1848 and served on the committee to build Rutland Town's East Parish meeting hall in 1853. He was also an organizer and officer of the Rutland Savings Bank, established in 1850. He was a trustee and

commissioner of the newly created Rutland Gas Light Company in 1856. Also like Proctor, the local level provided a springboard for state politics. Page served as Vermont's state treasurer throughout the Civil War from 1860 to 1866 and was governor from 1867 to 1868. His business interests included the presidency of the Rutland Railroad and the treasurer of the Howe Scale Company, the second-largest company in Rutland in the 1880s. He was a proponent for the expansion of Rutland Village and sought to reincorporate it as a city in 1880.

73. Hance, *History of Rutland, Vermont*, 532. In 1845, Barnes had employed only thirty-five workers; see Adams, *First Annual Report*, 43. In the state geologist's judgment, Barnes's and Dr. Sheldon's quarries had a hill with a "continuous range of marble which can never be exhausted."

74. Church Records of St. Bridget's Parish.

75. Hitchcock and others, *Report on the Geology of Vermont*, 981.

76. *Rutland Daily Herald*, January 12, 1880.

77. Ibid., December 23, 1872.

78. Klyza and Trombulak, *Story of Vermont*, 80.

79. U.S. Tenth Census, 1880, Population Manuscript for Rutland County; U.S. Tenth Census, 1880, Population Manuscript for Chittenden County.

Chapter 3

80. Ranging in a little over a decade, a cohort of future economic leaders was born: in 1831, Redfield Proctor and George Pullman; in 1834, Jim Fisk and Peter A.B. Widener; in 1835, Andrew Carnegie; in 1836, Jay Gould; in 1837, Charles Tyson Yerkes and J.P. Morgan; in 1838, James Keene and James J. Hill; in 1839, John D. Rockefeller; in 1840, H.H. Rogers and George F. Baker; in 1841, William Rockefeller and William C. Whitney; and in 1842, George Baer. On Redfield Proctor, see Bowie, "Redfield Proctor."

81. *Vermont Senate Journal*, 154; Bowie, "Redfield Proctor," 121.

82. Perhaps not a true partnership, attorneys in general frequently (then and now) enter into office relationships that are not binding but serve other useful purposes, such as shared expenses.

83. Cross, "Wheelock Graves Veazey," 37. Redfield Proctor was elected lieutenant governor in 1876 and governor of Vermont in 1878. Dunton was appointed to the Vermont Supreme Court in 1877. The *Rutland Directory* for 1878–79 lists only Veazey in a law office at 9 Merchants Row.

84. *Rutland Daily Herald*, February 1, 1868. Using CPI as the index, the $240,000 in 1867 would be $2,850,000 in 2001 purchasing power. Williamson, "What is the Relative Value?" Proctor's house was valued at $10,000 in 1867 according to the *Rutland Daily Herald*, February 1, 1868. Since 1868, much of the original land has been subdivided for further development. The house and the land are currently valued at $314,000, according to Rutland City Treasurer Ron Graves, interview with the author, May 6, 2002.

85. *Rutland Daily Herald*, January 21 and 22, 1868.

86. Ibid., January 21, 1868.

87. *Rutland Daily Herald*, February 1, 1868. See also French, *Proctor*, 45; this shows a picture of the second Redfield Proctor house decorated for President Harrison's visit on August 28, 1891. The first house had burned down in the previous decade.

88. *Rutland Daily Herald*, May 8, 1871.

89. For background on Proctor's skills, see Gale, *Proctor*, and Bowie, "Redfield Proctor," and for background on Barnes see Hance, *History of Rutland, Vermont*, 532. Bruce Laurie discusses the transformation from another perspective of the independent artisan into the worker. Barnes was closer to the artisan than Proctor with his sense of organization. See also Laurie, *Artisans into Workers*.

90. Proctor was part of a national movement that saw tariffs as a way of protecting and advancing American business interests. The high protection period was from 1861 to 1933. Senator Morrill from Vermont initiated the constant round of high tariffs. Certainly tariffs were issue beforehand in the tension between North and South, but now with the South's defection, high tariffs became the standard policy of the nation. See also Greene, ed. *Encyclopedia of American Political History*, 1263–66.

91. Similarly, Andrew Carnegie, in the midst of the panic of the 1870s that faced Proctor, built the Edgar Thompson Steel Works in Braddock and as a prudent risk-taker gambled his fortune on it. Proctor saw similar opportunities. Both thrived later when the economy and the demand for their products increased.

92. Gale, *Proctor*, 111.

93. According to John D. Andrews, who came to Proctor in 1876, the Sutherland Falls Marble Company owned one twelve-foot rubbing bed when he arrived. An expanded product line required more finishing capability. See also Gale, *Proctor*, 133.

94. *Rutland Daily Herald*, January 12, 1880.

95. *Rutland Daily Herald*, "Vermont's Marble Industry," January 12, 1880.

96. Ibid., January 31, 1880.

97. Ibid., July 15, 1880.

98. Ibid., January 31, 1880.

99. Ibid., September 30, 1880.

100. From Vermont Marble Company Directors Minutes, Vol. 1, 4–10, as also quoted in Bowie, "Redfield Proctor," unpublished doctoral dissertation, University of Wisconsin, 1980, 43. Using the CPI: $1,000 a month in 1880 would be $17,200 a month in 2001. Williamson, "What is the Relative Value?"

101. Gale, *Proctor*, 110.

102. Bowie, "Redfield Proctor," 49.

103. *Rutland Daily Herald*, "Vermont Marble Company Bonds," January 1, 1881. The CPI for $100 in 1881 would be valued at $1,720 in 2001, $500 in 1881 would be valued at $8,610 in 2001 and $1,000 in 1881 would be valued at $17,200 in 2001. Williamson, "What is the Relative Value?"

104. *Rutland Daily Herald*, December 9, 1880.

105. Ibid., January 31, 1881.

106. Gale, *Proctor*, 112.

107. The Producers' Marble cartel formed late in the year of 1880, one year after Proctor had formed the Vermont Marble Company. See also *Directory* for 1881–82.

108. *Rutland Daily Herald*, December 29, 1882.

109. As quoted in Bowie, "Redfield Proctor," 58.

110. Ibid., 43, from Vermont Marble Company Directors Minutes, Vol. 1, 4–10.

111. Bowie, "Redfield Proctor," 59.

112. Gino Ratti, "Cesare Ratti Family." In discussions with descendants of Italian marble workers who are now living in Center Rutland, they recalled how Italians from northern Italy were referred to as the Alta Italians to distinguish them from southern Italians. In Rutland, the two Italian communities had established two different Italian social and financial aid societies. Personal interviews, April 1997.

113. Hale, "Marble Valley's UN," 40.

114. *Rutland Daily Herald*, January 4, 1881.

115. Vermont Board of Railroad Commissioners, *Biennial Report of the Board*.

116. Based on the number of workers, its geographic distribution, its sales and the Industrial Census of 1900. See also Bowie, "Redfield Proctor."

CHAPTER 4

117. *Rutland Daily Herald*, "Wanted—Young Men," July 17, 1880.

118. Analysis of the U.S. Tenth Census, 1880, Population Manuscript for Rutland County.

119. Ibid.

120. Valentine, *Report of the Commissioner*. The report comments on the reliability of various immigrant groups.

121. *Rutland Daily Herald*, May 6, 1871.

122. U.S. Tenth Census, 1880, Population Manuscript for Rutland County.

123. Johnson, "Our Swedish Pioneers," 26.

124. Gale, *Proctor*, 134.

125. Ratti, "Cesare Ratti Family," 30.

126. Brayley, *History of the Granite Industry*, 36.

127. Italian Aid Society, *Italian Aid Society, 1894–1994*, 2. I also interviewed retired marble workers and their families in 1995 in their homes and other sites. In these interviews, I became aware of the self-defining term "Alta" for northern Italians. The Alta Italians saw themselves as quite distinctive from southern Italians. They were more skilled, such as carvers and marble workers. They were anticlerical and distrusted the Roman Church. Their cuisine was different; southern Italians were "spaghetti heads," derived from their frequent use of tomatoes in their meals.

128. Analysis of U.S. Census, 1880, Population for Rutland County and U.S. Census, 1900, Population for Rutland County.

129. *Commissioner's Report on Manufacturing and Agriculture*, 7–10, 15.

130. In St. Bridget's Parish of West Rutland's report to the Burlington Roman Catholic Diocese of Vermont in 1901, 338 Poles are indicated. In 1905, a separate parish, St. Stanislaus in West Rutland, was founded to service the growing Polish community. Report indicates that Father Mihulka as the pastor.

131. Redfield Proctor was aggressive in his concern for market share. In April 1881, for instance, he wrote to the manager of a distribution center in Toledo, Ohio: "You have got to strike in on trade in your territory with a vengeance and if you need another traveler [salesman], you must have him." Letter in the Proctor Collection at the Proctor Library, Proctor, Vermont. Distribution points were across the nation: "At the celebration of the Independence day, Wednesday, Fred Holden of Chicago, heretofore traveling salesman for the Chicago Marble Company was in town yesterday visiting his friends and bidding them adieu previous to his start on Saturday for San Francisco, where his headquarters will be in the future. Mr. Holden will travel through California selling marble for the Vermont Marble Company's San Francisco branch." *Rutland Daily Herald*, July 6, 1888.

132. *Rutland Daily Herald*, August 31, 1886.

133. Ibid., December 15, 1875, December 12, 1878, and December 6, 1883.

134. *Rutland Daily Herald*, "Earnings of Labor," Letter to the Editor, August 31, 1886. See also *Rutland Daily Herald*, May 17 and July 23, 1883, for further background on the workmen being paid once per month.

135. Hitchcock and others, *Report on the Geology of Vermont*, 757.

136. Robert Pye, director of the Marble Museum, interview with the author. I also visited the Slate Valley Museum in Granville, New York, to see such tools on display.

137. In the last decade of the twentieth century, a new method emerged. The marble worker can use an automatic channel burner. It is like a handheld burner but housed in a frame with an electric motor. The channel burner moves slowly down a track, making an even cut. Instead of a marble worker guiding the burner, a computer controls the machine.

138. Stone carvers, who earned wages comparable to doctors or lawyers at the turn of the century, were strong advocates of change in both labor and political movements. Before the advent of the Secret Service, stone carvers were the bodyguards for Abraham Lincoln during his 1861 inauguration. Stone carvers in the Chicago local were members of the first union in the country to get an eight-hour day in 1867.

139. In 1880, at a Republican caucus held in Rutland, speakers were brought in to support the issue of protective tariffs for American marble. See also *Rutland Daily Herald*, August 23, 1880.

140. Vermont Marble Company, *Work Rules*. The pamphlet has six pages of rules and stated that it was printed in American, Hungarian, Italian and Polish; the Representatives Plan was published in similar languages. Each had forty-six rules. The Representative Plan was also printed in Swedish. The pamphlet is located in the Vermont Historical Society Collection in Montpelier.

141. *Rutland Herald*, July 29, 1855; CIP index: $10,000 in 1855 would be $189,000 in 2001. Williamson, "What is Relative Value?"

142. *Rutland Daily Herald*, August 17, 1867.

143. Ibid., May 8, 1871. Barnes previously had represented Rutland in the state legislature for two years. Marble interests and political interests were often intertwined.

144. *Rutland Daily Herald*, September 13, 1892.

145. Ibid., February 13, 1893.

146. Ibid. The *Herald* mistakenly refers to Kulig as Sulig.

147. *Rutland Daily Herald*, July 26, 1893.

148. Sarca, "A Heritage Revealed," 6.

149. *Rutland Daily Herald*, September 25, 1880.

150. *Burlington Free Press*, May 18, 1892.

151. *Rutland Daily Herald*, February 18, 1893.

152. Ibid., July 26, 1888.
153. Ibid., February 15, 1906.
154. Ibid., August 6, 1902.
155. Ibid., July 7, 1904.
156. Ibid., February 17, 1906.
157. Ibid., February 20, 1906, November 30, 1907, and December 5, 1907.

CHAPTER 5

158. *Rutland Daily Herald*, "Swedish Colony's History Traced," from Proctor Free Library scrapbook, Proctor, Vermont. The term "tenement" at that time did not have the negative connotation that it has today.
159. Many of the Irish marble workers lived on Barrett's Hill in Rutland. This section of Rutland has a sign, unlike other sections, marking its location.
160. *Harper's New Monthly Magazine*, "A Vacation in Vermont," 827.
161. Hannon, *History of West Rutland*, 58.
162. Letter in *Rutland Courier* on Friday, May 6, 1859, from a marble worker.
163. Johnson, "Our Swedish Pioneers," 24–27.
164. Harold Billings, interview on Pollution in the Valley, July 1997. As a young man growing up in the 1950s, Billings can recall the air pollution from the railroad trains going through West Rutland. By then, the marble industry and the railroads had long passed their peak period of the early 1900s, when air pollution in the valley was more extensive.
165. *Rutland Daily Herald*, September 10, 1881.
166. Ibid., March 27, 1882.
167. Ibid., February 25, 1909.
168. Ibid., July 3, 1894.
169. Hance, "Hospital Care in Rutland," 14.
170. Stewart, "Beginning of Industrial Nursing," 4, 71.
171. *Rutland Directory, 1891–1892*, 65, 89, 99, 159, 165, 167, 173, 181, 217, 225–26, 245, 246; *Rutland Directory, 1895–1896*.
172. Caverly, "Preliminary Report of an Epidemic," in *Infantile Paralysis in Vermont*, 15–20.
173. Ibid., 23.
174. Ibid., 176.
175. Ibid., 55.

CHAPTER 6

176. *Rutland Daily Herald* on July 18, 1878, commented on the possible division: "There is some talk of dividing the town between East and

West sides, into Rutland and West Rutland. The people in the west part of the town are generally in favor of the division we understand. The West village has all the advantages of a center of population and business, and if a satisfactory division of the property and liabilities of the town could be made, and dividing line could be satisfactorily decided upon, there would be many reasons why a division of the town would be desirable."

177. The argument of geography was an argument of convenience and of progress beyond the village of Rutland. Voting would be accessible and bring about more local control rather than being subservient to the village. But there were also economic issues, such as access to banks. Proctor later would provide a bank for his workers. He would also be a founding member of the Marble Savings Bank. Shopping was another issue. Workers protested that traveling to Rutland Village, where many of the shops were located, was nearly an all-day trip. Thus, from the workers' viewpoints, the division of Rutland into smaller towns would provide a better quality of life by bringing about more local control of resources and not concentrating wealth and resources in only one section of the town.

178. Both Redfield Proctor and Charles Clement, the patriarchs of their powerful families, migrated to Rutland. Charles Clement grew up in Bridgewater, Vermont. As part of the outward migration affecting Vermont in the middle decades of the nineteenth century, he sought more financial opportunity in the Midwest and moved to Alton, Illinois, where he was one of the volunteers who periodically protected Edward Lovejoy, the abolitionist printer in the town. The family estate was built by Charles Clement in 1856–57: Clementwood, in Center Rutland on Clement Road. Charles and his wife, Elizabeth, had eight children, but only three of them survived: Wallace, born in 1835; Percival, in 1846; and Waldo, in 1851. The sons along with their father used the money from the marble investments to move into banking, investments and, in the case of Percival, journalism, politics and railroads. Sherman, *Clements of Haverhill and Rutland*. Copy located in the Vermont Room of the Rutland Library. The industrial leaders in the Gilded Age came overwhelmingly from families of upper- or middle-class status. See also Sawyer "American Historians and the Business Elite," 309–328.

179. *Rutland Daily Herald*, April 30, 1881.

180. Child, *Gazetteer and Business Directory*, 467, 425, 433.

181. Beers 1854 Map in the Special Collections of Rutland Historical Society, Rutland, Vermont.

182. McKinney, comp., *Industrial Advantages of the State of Vermont*, 31.

183. Resch, *Bob Mitchell Years*.
184. The family used the money from their marble company when they sold it to diversify their financial interests. The three surviving children—Wallace, Percival and Waldo—along with their father, were involved in the family concerns. Percival was the leader in the younger generation.
185. *Rutland Daily Herald*, June 8, 1867.
186. Ibid., July 19, 1880; *Annual Report for Rutland, 1886 and 1887*; Conant, *Geography, History, Constitution*, 103.
187. The petition argued that the "Petioners are Principly of Simelar Sentements in matters of [Religion]…the Central Part of the Town of Rutland for some Thousands of Acres, is barran, Unarrable Land and Probably never will be Cultivated or improved…that a Large number of its inhabitants both in the Easterly and Westerly Parts must be put to Excessive Lengths of Travil to Convene in the Center…and the Town…have had Several meetings…to build a Meeting house… nigh the Center…but never Could be so happy as to agree…we most Earnestly Pray your Honors…[to] Grant…the Town of Rutland be Divided into two Societies." Hoyt, *General Petitions*, 293–94.
188. *Rutland Daily Herald*, July 18, 1878.
189. Ibid., December 6, 1880.
190. The contents of the Grand List "of a town shall contain among other things the following particulars: 1) the name of each taxpayer; 2) the post office address of all taxpayers and corporations having taxable property in the town, provided the same are known to the listers; 3) a brief description and the listed valuation of each separate piece or parcel of taxable property in the town, owned by each taxpayer and the total value of all such real estate not exempt from taxation; 4) the listed valuation of such taxpayer's personal estate taxable in the town; 5 a) separate columns which will show the approximate acreage of woodland, cropland, and pasture land; 5 b) the director shall make such rules and regulations as shall adequately define, for the benefit of listers and for the promotion of a uniform procedure, what constitutes woodland, cropland and pasture land as used in this subdivision." *Vermont Statutes Annotated, Title 32, Sections 1-5978*, 385–86.
191. *Rutland Daily Herald*, December 6, 1880.
192. Ibid., November 15, 1880.
193. "No. 222: An Act to Incorporate the Village of Proctor, 191. Although both bills were passed in the same day of November 11, 1883 the influential power of Proctor was shown in the order of the priority. The vote for division of Proctor was Bill 17 and for West Rutland was Bill 23," from *Acts and Resolves Passed*, 191.
194. Ibid.

195. *Rutland Daily Herald*, May 5 and 12, 1864.

196. Ibid., April 16, May 20, May 22 and June 12, 1868.

197. Ibid., March 4, 1880; See also *Rutland Daily Herald*, March 2 and 3, 1880.

198. *Rutland Daily Herald*, August 4, 1882, and January 30, 1884.

199. Ibid., March 25, 1882.

200. Ibid., December 17, 1880.

201. Ibid., December 17, 1881. A hundred couples attended out of nearly a thousand workers. For the importance of worker culture in providing a social bonding for political action, see Gutman, *Work, Culture, and Society*, especially 211–60, which examines the myth of the rags-to-riches ethos.

202. *Rutland Daily Herald*, August 27, 1886.

203. Montgomery, *Workers Control in America*, 20.

204. *Rutland Daily Herald*, March 3, 1887; see also *Rutland Daily Herald*, February 25, 1887.

205. *Rutland Daily Herald*, August 27, 1886.

206. Ibid., August 27, September 6 and October 6, 1886.

207. Ibid., August 31, 1886.

208. Ibid.

209. Ibid.

210. Ibid., August 27, 1886.

211. Ibid., September 7, 1886.

212. Ibid.

213. Ibid., September 8, 1886.

214. Ibid.

215. Ibid. The *Herald* entitled the article "Rutland's Quake," a reference to a South American earthquake that had recently left much destruction. The reference was not lost on the business community.

216. Ibid.

217. Ibid.

218. Ibid.

219. Ibid., September 15, 1886.

220. Ibid., October 6, 1886.

221. Ibid.

222. *Hearing Before the Legislative Committee.*

223. *Rutland Daily Herald*, August 2, 1893. Ripley and others recounted the issues of division in 1886.

224. Ibid., November 2, 1886; Another instance of Percival Clement's obsession with the Proctors also occurred in late 1885. Clement bought the Merchants Row building at the intersection of Evelyn Street and Merchants Row in the center of the business district for $18,000.

Clement wrote to his father, "I have bought the old bank building. I was afraid that Proctor with whom they had been talking would give them that [$18,000] when he should know that I was after it." Clement continually perceived the Proctors as his nemeses. Letter from Percival Clement to Charles Clement, December 29, 1885, in Resch, *Rutland Herald History*, 65.

225. Bearse, ed., *Vermont: A Guide to the Green Mountain State*, 334.
226. *Hearing Before the Legislative Committee.*
227. H. 17, Act 137, "An Act to Incorporate the Town of Proctor," November 18, 1886; H. 23, Act 138, "An Act to Incorporate the Town of West Rutland," November 19, 1886.
228. Kathy Watters, administrative assistant archivist, Vermont State Archives, Montpelier, Vermont, interview with the author. See also *Rutland Daily Herald*, November 18, 1886; *Vermont Journal* (1886): 190, 193, 199, 205.
229. *Rutland Daily Herald*, November 18, 1886.
230. *Rutland Daily Herald*, February 28, 1887.
231. Ibid., March 1, 1887; for the candidates' occupations, see Pelton, *Pelton's Directory, 1887–1888.*
232. *Rutland Daily Herald*, March 1, 1887.
233. Ibid.
234. Ibid., March 2, 1887.
235. Ibid., March 10, 1887.
236. Ibid.
237. Ibid. See also March 2 and 10, 1887, and February 24 and October 26, 1888. After the Haymarket Affair (1886), there was increased fear of radicalism and anarchists. The Knights of Labor were perceived to be radical, and now they were in Rutland. They sought change and reform, and since many of their constituents in Rutland were first- and second-generation immigrants, the threat was perceived as more acute.
238. Sherman, *Rutland Free Library*, 17–18.
239. *Rutland Daily Herald*, March 19, 1887.
240. Ibid., March 31, 1887.
241. U.S. Congress, Senate Immigration Committee, "Immigration Abuses," 4–7. Morrill argued that a large influx of uneducated foreigners would lower the general level of literacy in the United States. He had sponsored the first bill for establishing the land grant college system in 1862, and in 1890, the second Morrill Act provided long-term financing for that system.
242. *Rutland Daily Herald*, March 2, 10, 1887, and February 24 and October 26, 1888.

243. Ibid., March 7, 1888.
244. Ibid.
245. Ibid.
246. Ibid.
247. Ibid., March 8, 1888.

CHAPTER 7

248. Lyman W. Redington's family background included a grandfather who fought in the Revolution and a father who was a lawyer and a judge in St. Lawrence County, New York, to where the father had migrated from Vergennes, Vermont. The father was quite successful with lumber mills and was highly respected. The father was also a staunch Democrat. Lyman's mother was a sister of Charles Sheldon, of the Sheldon and Sons Marble Company, and thus connected with the upper echelons of Rutland society. In 1878, Lyman was elected to the legislature and was the Democratic nominee for House Speaker. In 1884, he was the attorney for Rutland.

249. Gale, *Proctor*, 115. See also Dillingham, *Redfield Proctor*. Dillingham also acknowledges that Proctor was the head of the Republican Party in the state from the time when Proctor was governor. In the cabinet, Proctor used his organizational skills to bring about changes in the department, as he had done at the Vermont Marble Company. In a memorial address to the Senate on January 9, 1909, commemorating Proctor's achievements, his fellow senator from Vermont at the turn of the century, William Paul Dillingham, recounted Proctor's achievement as secretary of war. When Proctor came into office, necessary information pertaining to "military and medical records for the adjustment of pensions, pay bounty, and other claims of soldiers, their widows, and orphans—was hopelessly in arrears," 16. Encountering resistance and prophecies of disaster for the department, Proctor streamlined its organization for more effective communication. He consolidated fourteen different divisions of the department into one.

250. Johnson, ed., *Historic Architecture of Rutland County*, 281.

251. McKinney, *Industrial Advantages of the State of Vermont*, 12.

252. Ibid.

253. Dillingham, *Address Before the Opening of the Vermont Legislature*, Vermont Historical Society Special Collections. When Dillingham was the U.S. senator from Vermont, he became one of the national leaders in attempting to restrict immigration. Vermont has a small population, but the perception of the danger reflected the concerns of larger

states. John Higham considers Dillingham a "moderate restrictionist." Nevertheless, Dillingham's leadership tried to shape the national agenda. See also Higham, *Strangers in the Land*, 310.

254. A team of social scientists studied "good" and "bad" families over a twelve-year period in Vermont and suggested which families need to be eliminated. The study culminated in a report issued to policymakers and led to the Vermont legislature passing a 1931 sterilization law. The law permitted the state to sterilize several hundred poor and rural Vermont citizens, Abenaki and others whom the state judged, based on the criteria of the study, unworthy to procreate. Dr. Henry Perkins of the University of Vermont catalogued a list of "pedigrees of degeneracy." Vermont became the thirty-first state to legalize sterilization of the handicapped or the "feeble-minded." See also Gallagher, *Breeding Better Vermonters*.

255. Robinson, *Vermont*, see especially 300–307, 328–30 and 365.

256. See also Dillingham's farewell address to the Vermont legislature in 1890, *Vermont State Journal*.

257. Ibid.

258. Immigration Commission, *Dictionary of Race and Peoples*, 120; *New York Times*, "U.S. Senator Dillingham on Tour of Europe," August 13, 1907, 13. For an account of Governor Dillingham's selection of Swedish immigrants as the preferred immigrant group, see Valentine, *Report of the Commissioner*, and *Vermont Senate Journal*, 1888–90.

259. Immigration Commission, *Abstracts of the Reports*, 288.

260. *Rutland Daily Herald*, September 8, 1892.

261. Ibid., November 21, 1892.

262. *Rutland Directory, 1895–1896*, 298.

263. Rezneck, "Unemployment, Unrest, and Relief," 324–25.

264. *Rutland Daily Herald*, September 22, 1892.

265. Ibid., July 5, 1893.

266. Hofstadter, *Great Issues in American History*, Vol. III, *From Reconstruction to the Present Day, 1864–1981*, 144; "Omaha Platform."

267. *Rutland Daily Herald*, July 28, 1893.

268. *Rutland Historical Quarterly* 12, no. 2, "Rutland's Mayors," (Spring 1982): 19; *Rutland Daily Herald*, March 7, 1894, and June 28, 1915.

269. *Rutland Daily Herald*, March 7, 1894.

270. Ibid., January 3, 17 and 18, 1894, and February 7, 1895.

271. Ibid., January 3, 17 and 18, 1894, and March 6, 1895.

272. Herndon, comp., *Men of Progress*, 215–17; *Rutland Daily Herald*, March 6, 1895. He died at age sixty-nine on August 14, 1904, from complications of a stroke. He was a resident of Rutland for more than forty years. See also *Rutland Daily Herald*, August 15, 1904.

273. *Rutland Daily Herald*, March 2, 1896.
274. Browne had added an "e" to his name by this time.
275. *Rutland Daily Herald*, October 6, 1896.
276. Ibid., October 13, 1896.
277. Ibid., October 29, 1896.
278. Ibid., November 17, 1896.
279. Ibid.
280. Ibid.
281. Ibid., February 9, 1897.
282. Ibid., February 11, 1897.
283. Ibid., February 12, 1897.
284. Ibid., February 11, 1897.
285. *Rutland Historical Quarterly*, "Rutland's Mayors," 20.

Chapter 8

286. *Rutland Historical Quarterly*, "Rutland's Mayors," 21.
287. Johnson, *Nineteen-Six in Vermont*, 181.
288. Clement, "Dangers of Centralization," 1–7. Pamphlet available in Vermont Collections at Middlebury College, Vermont.
289. Green, *Nineteen-Two*, 86–87.
290. Johnson, *Nineteen-Six in Vermont*, 163–64. Includes election results for 1902 and 1906. See also Office of the Vermont Secretary of State, Vermont State Archives website.
291. *Rutland Daily Herald*, July 7, 1904.
292. Ibid., July 12, 1904.
293. Ibid., July 13, 1904.
294. Ibid., July 27, 1904.
295. Ibid., August 3, 1904.
296. Ibid., August 8, 1904.
297. Ibid., August 16 and 17, 1904.
298. Ibid., September 23, 1904.
299. Ibid.
300. Johnson, *Nineteen-Six in Vermont*, 15.
301. The full text of his responses is quoted in Johnson, *Nineteen-Six in Vermont*, 14–16.
302. *Rutland Daily Herald*, July 29, 1906.
303. Ibid., June 10, 1912.
304. Stewart, "Beginning of Industrial Nursing," 69.
305. Brochure on dedication of Mortimer R. Proctor Room, September 1969, in Proctor Free Library, Proctor, Vermont.

306. Johnson, *Proctor*, 13.

307. Stewart, "Beginning of Industrial Nursing," 73.

308. Rose, *Emily Dutton Proctor*. Contains three essays by Rose, a companion, to Margaret Proctor Kelley and Reverend Ben Roberts, who gave the sermon. Unpaginated. The pamphlet is located in the Vermont Room of Castleton State College; *Rutland Daily Herald*, July 29, 1906.

309. Davies, Armitage, Blittersdorf and Harvie, *Pittsford's Second Century*, 258.

310. Rose, *Emily Dutton Proctor*.

311. *Rutland Daily Herald*, December 17, 1948.

312. Caverly, *Thirteenth (Third Biennial) Report*.

313. Ellis, "Cavendish House," 91–92.

314. Gale, *Proctor*, 226–27.

315. Perkins, *Report of the State Geologist*, 329.

316. Ibid., 253; see also Leland, "Barre," 25.

317. United States Department of the Interior, *Granite Cutting*, 234–35. Special Collections of the Vermont Marble Museum and Special Collection of the Aldrich Museum in Barre, Vermont, which contains records of the Rock of Ages granite workers.

318. *Rutland Daily Herald*, November 4, 1935.

319. Ibid., November 5, 1935.

320. Ibid., November 8, 1935.

321. *Rutland Daily Herald*, "17 Hurt in Bloody Strike Melee, 5 Men in Hospital," January 8, 1936; *Rutland Daily Herald*, "W. Rutland Voters Ask [Governor] Smith to Aid in Ending Strike," February 22, 1936.

322. See *Rutland Daily Herald*, November 10, 1935, for the company's securing of police officers to protect its property.

323. *Rutland Daily Herald*, November 10, 1935.

324. Ibid., November 17, 1935.

325. Ibid., November 23, 1935.

326. Ibid., November 28, 1935.

327. Ibid., January 7, 1936.

328. *Rutland Daily Herald*, "Selectman Guilty of Refusing Relief," January 13, 1936. A jury found Dwyer guilty of "willful neglect of his duty" to provide clothing for schoolchildren of two families of marble workers.

329. *Rutland Daily Herald*, February 21, 1936.

330. Ibid., February 25, 1936; *Rutland Daily Herald*, March 5, 1936.

331. *Rutland Daily Herald*, July 30, 1936; see also *Brattleboro Reformer*, February 2 and April 2, 1937.

332. *Rutland Daily Herald* April, 17, 18 and 29, 1936.

333. Ibid., April 27, 1936.

334. Ibid.

335. Ibid., May 31, 1936. For national perspective on the strike, see Marburg, "Struggle in Marble," 413–14, and *New Republic*, "A Strike in Vermont," 155.

336. Judd, *New Deal in Vermont*, 144. The work was originally the author's thesis at Harvard, 1959.

337. Schulberg, *Writers in America*, 50. Archibald MacLeish was also on a committee that supported the strike. See also *New Republic*, "A Strike in Vermont," 155.

338. *Rutland Daily Herald*, July 2, 1936.

339. Ibid., July 27, 1936.

340. *Brattleboro Reformer*, February 2 and April 2, 1937.

341. For early background about Partridge, see Herndon, *Men of Progress*, 209–210.

342. Redfield Proctor Jr. was the youngest of the five children of Redfield and Emily Proctor and was born in 1879. Rose, *Emily Dutton Proctor*; for Partridge and Proctor's position as president and vice-president, see *Rutland, West Rutland, Proctor Directory, 1935*, 420–21. Mortimer Proctor, Redfield Jr.'s son, was assistant superintendent of the marble company.

343. Krause, *Battle for Homestead*. Partridge played a similar role to that of F.C. Dumaine at the Amoskeag Mills in Manchester, New Hampshire. The Vermont Marble Company strike of 1935–36 ended the trusting bond between the worker and the company, similar to the mills of Amoskeag at Manchester, New Hampshire. See Harveven, *Family Time and Industrial Time*, for a discussion of a similar situation occurring in New Hampshire.

344. For recent changes regarding Vermont politics and government, economic conditions and social conditions, see Sherman, *Fast Lane on a Dirt Road*; Conroy, *Challenging the Boundaries of Reform*; Sherman, ed., *Vermont State Government Since 1965*; Guma, *People's Republic*; and Kunin, *Living a Political Life*.

CONCLUSION

345. *Fifty-Ninth Annual Report of Officers: Sutherland Community Center, 1903–1946*.

346. Gale, *Proctor*, 119.

347. Carder became mayor in 1904. There were still deep divisions in the Republican Party between the Clement and Proctor wing and their allies. The workers sought someone who would more closely represent their voice in the public forum.

348. Articles of the United Committee to Aid the Vermont Marble Workers, findings appeared in Marburg, "Struggle in Marble," and *New Republic*, "A Strike in Vermont."

349. As quoted in Barber, *An Aristocracy of Everyone*, 247.

350. Bailey, "Rock Steady," 14.

351. Gawett, interview with the author, May 2000.

352. Gottfried Pleiss founded OMYA in 1884 in Switzerland. In 1891, he acquired the second site for the company in Omey, France. Because of the loyal relationship of the residents to the company, the company adopted the name OMYA. "On the same day he married Emma Staufer, August 24, 1884, Gottfried Plüss founded the Plüss-Staufer company in Oftringen, Switzerland. To keep his promise to his customers 'to manufacture glazier's putty of highest quality,' Gottfried purchased a site in the Champayne District of France in 1891 for its deposits of high quality ore. A second location purchased in Omey, France became the site of a new factory that began production in 1900. The OMYA name and logo, now familiar around the world, were in fact inspired by the loyal relationship with 'Les Omyats,' the residents of Omey. And these ore deposits still set the standards for raw materials used to produce the highest quality OMYA ground calcium carbonate products." For recent information about the company and its moving its headquarters from Vermont to Cincinnati, see www.omyainvermont.org.

353. Harris, interview with the author.

354. *Rutland Daily Herald*, July 22, 2002.

BIBLIOGRAPHY

Primary Sources

Acts and Resolves Passed by the General Assembly of the State of Vermont, at the Eighth Biennial Session, 1884. Rutland, VT: Tuttle & Company, 1885.

Adams, C.B. *First Annual Report of the Geology of the State of Vermont.* Burlington, VT: Chauncey Goodrich, 1845.

Annual Report of the Town of Rutland, Year Ending February 25, 1887. Town of Rutland, Vermont. Rutland, VT: Tuttle & Company, 1887. Records available at the Rutland Historical Society.

Beers 1854 map. Special Collections of Rutland Historical Society, Rutland, Vermont.

Bennett, William. *Narrative of a Recent Journey of Six Weeks in Ireland.* London: C. Gilpin, 1847.

Bibbens, Katie. "On Work." Plaque in the Graduation Program Castleton State Normal School in the Woodruff Administration Building of Castleton State College, June 27, 1878.

Billings, Harold. Interview on pollution in the valley, July 1997.

Brochure on dedication of Mortimer R. Proctor Room, September 1969. Located in Proctor Free Library, Proctor, Vermont.

Caverly, Charles, MD, President of Board. *Thirteenth (Third Biennial) Report of the State Board of Health of the State of Vermont from January 1, 1900 to December 31, 1901.* Rutland, VT: Tuttle & Company, 1901.

Child, Hamilton. *Gazetteer and Business Directory of Rutland County, VT, 1881–1882*. Syracuse, NY: Journal Office, 1881.

Church Records of St. Bridget's Parish. West Rutland: Roman Catholic Diocese of Vermont. All records submitted annually from 1860 to present.

Clement, Percival W. "Dangers of Centralization in Governmental Functions and Activities Held at the Governors; Conference at Harrisburg, Pa, December the Second, Nineteen Hundred Twenty." Rutland, VT: P.W. Clement, 1920, 1–7. Pamphlet available in Vermont Collections at Middlebury College, Vermont.

Commissioner's Report on Manufacturing and Agriculture. Montpelier, VT, 1890.

Dwight, Timothy. *Travels through the State of North America and the Province of Upper Canada During the Years 1795, 1796, and 1797*. London, 1823.

Fifty-Ninth Annual Report of Officers: Sutherland Community Center, 1903–1946. From Proctor Library scrapbook, clipping dated 1946.

"First Constitution," Chapter 1, Section 3 in *Vermont State Papers*. Middlebury, VT: J.W. Copeland, 1823.

Gawett, Stanley, Owner of Gawett Marble. Interview with the author in May 2000.

Harris, Christie, Public Relations Officer of OMYA. Interview with the author in Florence, Vermont, on October 18, 2002.

Hitchcock, Edward, and Edward Hitchcock Jr., Albert D. Hager and Charles Hitchcock. *Report on the Geology of Vermont: Descriptive, Theoretical, Economical, and Scenographical*. Claremont, NH: Claremont Manufacturing Company, 1861.

Hoyt, Edward A., ed. *General Petitions, 1778–1787*. Vol. 8. Montpelier, VT: Vermont Secretary of State, 1952.

Immigration Commission. *Abstracts of the Reports of the Immigration Commission*. Washington, D.C.: Government Printing Office, 1911.

———. *Dictionary of Race and Peoples*. Washington, D.C.: Government Printing Office, n.d.

New Republic 86. "A Strike in Vermont" (March 18, 1936): 155.

Pelton, George E., ed. *Pelton's Directory, 1887–1888: A Complete Register of the Residents, Business Houses and Manufacturing Firms of the Three Towns of Rutland, West Rutland and Proctor*. Rutland, VT: Rutland Pelton Printing Company, 1887.

Perkins, George. *Report of the State Geologist on the Mineral Industries and Geology of Vermont, 1921–1922*. Burlington, VT: Free Press Printing Company, 1923.

Pye, Robert, of the Vermont Marble Museum. Interview with the author in Proctor, Vermont, on May, 24, 2000.

R.S. Dillon & Company, comp. *Rutland Directory, 1878–1879.* Village of Rutland, Center Rutland and West Rutland. Rutland, VT: Tuttle & Company, n.d.

Rutland Daily Herald. "Earnings of Labor." Letter to the Editor. August 31, 1886.

———. "Selectman Guilty of Refusing Relief." January 13, 1936.

———. "17 Hurt in Bloody Strike Melee, 5 Men in Hospital." January 8, 1936.

———. "Swedish Colony's History Traced." n.d.

———. "Vermont Marble Company Bonds." January 1, 1881.

———. "Vermont's Marble Industry." January 12, 1880.

———. "Wanted—Young Men." July 17, 1880.

———. "W. Rutland Voters Ask [Governor] Smith to Aid in Ending Strike." February 22, 1936.

Rutland Directory, 1895–1896. Rutland, VT: Tuttle & Company, 1895.

Rutland, West Rutland, Proctor Directory, 1935. Rutland, VT: Tuttle & Company, n.d.

State of Vermont. *Hearing Before the Legislative Committee on the Incorporation of the Town of Proctor: Examination in the Case of the Division of Rutland.* Taken at Proctor, Vermont, on Tuesday morning, November 2, 1886, published in 1887, State Archives. Rutland, VT: Tuttle & Company, 1888.

Stewart, Ada Mayo. "The Beginning of Industrial Nursing in Vermont." *Rutland Historical Society Quarterly* 25, no. 4 (1995). Stewart's original comments later reprinted.

United States Department of the Interior. *Granite Cutting: An Analysis of the Granite Cutter's Trade.* Washington, D.C.: Government Printing Office, 1938, 234–35. Special Collections of the Vermont Marble Museum and Special Collection of the Aldrich Museum in Barre, Vermont, which contains records of the Rock of Ages granite workers.

U.S. Census, 1860. Washington, D.C.: Government Printing Office.

U.S. Census of Manufacturing, 1850. Washington, D.C.: Government Printing Office.

U.S. Census. Population for Rutland County, 1880. Washington, D.C.: U.S. National Archives, microfilm.

U.S. Census. Population for Rutland County, 1900. Washington, D.C.: U.S. National Archives, microfilm.

U.S. Congress, Senate Immigration Committee. "Immigration Abuses, Remarks of Justin S. Morrill of Vermont in the Senate of the United States, December 14, 1887 on His Bill to Regulate Immigration." Washington, D.C.: Government Printing Office, 1887.

U.S. First Census, 1791. Population Manuscript for Rutland County, Vermont. Washington, D.C.: U.S. National Archives, microfilm.

U.S. Second Census, 1800. Population Manuscript for Rutland County, Vermont. Washington, D.C.: U.S. National Archives, microfilm.

U.S. Seventh Census, 1850. Industrial Manuscript Records of the Census of Industry. Washington, D.C.: U.S. National Archives and Records Service for Rutland County, microfilm.

U.S. Seventh Census, 1850. Population for Chittenden County, Vermont. Washington, D.C.: U.S. National Archives. Microfilm.

U.S. Tenth Census, 1880. Population Manuscript for Chittenden County, Vermont. Washington, D.C.: U.S. National Archives, microfilm.

U.S. Tenth Census, 1880. Population Manuscript for Rutland County, Vermont. Washington, D.C.: U.S. National Archives, microfilm.

U.S. Third Census, 1810. Population Manuscript for Rutland Census. Washington, D.C.: U.S. National Archives, microfilm.

Valentine, Alonzo B. *Report of the Commissioner of Agriculture and Manufacturing Interests in State of Vermont, 1889–1890*. Rutland, VT: Tuttle & Company, 1890.

Vermont Board of Railroad Commissioners. *Biennial Report of the Board of Railroad Commissioners of the State of Vermont*. Boston, MA: Rand Avery Company, 1888.

Vermont Bureau of Publicity. *Industrial Vermont: The Mineral, Manufacturing, and Water Power Resources of the Green Mountain State*. Essex Junction: Vermont Bureau of Publicity, 1850.

Vermont Journal. H. 17, Act 137. "An Act to Incorporate the Town of Proctor," Vermont State Archives, November 18, 1886.

———. H. 23, Act 138. "An Act to Incorporate the Town of West Rutland," Vermont State Archives, November 19, 1886.

Vermont Marble Company Directors Minutes, Vol. 1. www.vermonthistory. org/documents/findaid/vmctreas.pdf.

Vermont Marble Company. *Work Rules*. Proctor: Vermont Marble Company, n.d. Pamphlet is in the Vermont Historical Society Collection in Montpelier.

Vermont Senate Journal, 1874. Rutland, VT: Tuttle & Company, 1877.

Vermont Senate Journal, 1888–90. Rutland, VT: Tuttle & Company, n.d.

Vermont Statutes Annotated, Title 32, Sections 1-5978. Salem, NH: Butterworth Legal Publishers, 1994.

Watters, Kathy, Administrative Assistant Archivist, Vermont State Archives, Montpelier, Vermont. Interview with the author, n.d.

Newspapers

Brattleboro Reformer, 1937.

Burlington Free Press, 1892.

Rutland County Independent, 1872.

Rutland Herald, 1835, 1837, 1843, 1846, 1855, 1859, 1864, 1867–68, 1871–72, 1875, 1878, 1880–84, 1886–88, 1892–97, 1902, 1904, 1906–7, 1912, 1915, 1935–36 and 2002.

SECONDARY SOURCES

Albers, Jan. *Hands on the Land: History of the Vermont Landscape.* Cambridge, MA: MIT Press, 2000.

Bailey, Craig. "Rock Steady." *Business Digest* 15, no. 9 (February 1999).

Balivet, Robert. "Vermont Sheep Industry: 1811–1880." *Vermont History* 33, no. 1 (1965).

Barber, Benjamin R. *An Aristocracy of Everyone: The Politics of Education and the Future of America.* New York: Oxford University Press, 1992.

Batchellear, Albert. *New Hampshire Grants: The Charter of Townships.* Concord, NH: Edward Pearson, public printer, 1895.

Bearse, Ray, ed. *Vermont: A Guide to the Green Mountain State.* Boston, MA: Houghton Mifflin, 1968.

Bowie, Chester Winston. "Redfield Proctor: A Biography." Madison: University of Wisconsin–Madison, 1980.

Braisli, Gibbs, Reverend. "Baptist." *The Churches of Rutland.* Rutland, VT: Brehmen Brothers, 1900.

Brayley, Arthur W. *History of the Granite Industry of New England.* Vol. II. Boston, MA: National Association of Granite Industries, 1913.

Caverly, A.M. *History of the Town of Pittsford, Vermont, with Biographical Sketches.* Rutland, VT: Tuttle & Company, 1872.

Caverly, Charles S., MD. "Preliminary Report of an Epidemic of Paralytic Disease Occurring in Vermont, in the Summer of 1894," in *Yale Journal* (November 1894) as reprinted in *Infantile Paralysis in Vermont, 1894–1922.* Burlington, VT: State Department of Public Health, 1924.

Collins, Edward Day. *A History of Vermont: With Geological and Geographical Notes, Bibliography, Chronology, Maps and Illustrations.* Boston, MA: Ginn and Company, 1903.

Conant, Edward. *Geography, History, Constitution and Civil Government of Vermont.* Rutland, VT: Tuttle & Company, 1925.

Conroy, W.J. *Challenging the Boundaries of Reform: Socialism in Burlington.* Philadelphia, PA: Temple University Press, 1990.

Cross, David. "Wheelock Graves Veazey." *Rutland Historical Society Quarterly* 25, no. 2 (1995).

Davidson, James. "On East and West Parish." Interview with the author, October 2009.

Davies, Joan S., Margaret Armitage, Lois Blittersdorf and Jan Harvie. *Pittsford's Second Century, 1872–1997.* West Kennebunk, ME: Phoenix Publishing, 1998.

Dillingham, William Paul. *Address Before the Opening of the Vermont Legislature, 1888.* Vermont Historical Society Special Collections, Montpelier, Vermont.

———. "Farewell Address." *Vermont State Journal* (1890).

———. *Redfield Proctor: Memorial Address.* Washington, D.C.: Government Printing Office, 1909.

Doyle, William. *Vermont Political Tradition and Those Who Helped Make It.* Montpelier, VT: Doyle Publisher, 2000.

Dunn, Mary Lee. "On Irish Emigration." Interview with the author regarding her research for her master's thesis at the University of Massachusetts, July 3, 2002.

Ellis, Helen. "Cavendish House." *Vermonter* 22 (1918): 5–6.

French, Ruth. *Proctor: The Way It Was.* Poultney, VT: Journal Press, 1975.

Gale, David. *Proctor: The Story of a Marble Town.* Brattleboro: Vermont Printing Company, 1922.

Gallagher, Nancy. *Breeding Better Vermonters: The Eugenics Project in the Green Mountain State.* Hanover: University Press of New England, 1999.

Gilmore, Robert C. "Connecticut and the Foundation of Vermont." PhD dissertation, Yale University, 1953.

Greene, Jack P., ed. *Encyclopedia of American Political History: Studies of the Principal Movements and Ideas.* 3 vols. New York: Charles Scribner's Sons, 1984.

Green, Mason A. *Nineteen-two in Vermont: The Fight for Local Option, Ten Years After.* Rutland, VT: Marble City Press, 1912.

Guma, Greg. *The People's Republic: Vermont and the Sanders Revolution.* Shelburne, VT: New England Press, 1989.

Gutman, Herbert G. *Work, Culture, and Society in Industrializing America: Essays in American Working-Class and Social History.* New York: Alfred A. Knopf, 1976.

Hale, Elizabeth. "Marble Valley's UN." *American Heritage* 2 (Spring 1951).

Hance, Dawn. *The History of Rutland, Vermont, 1761–1861.* Rutland, VT: Academy Press, 1991.

———. "Hospital Care in Rutland: The First Century." *Rutland Historical Quarterly* 26, no. 1 (1996): 14.

Hands, T. "An Emigrant's Chances in New Hampshire, 1821." *Monthly Magazine* (September 1821). Republished in *Magazine of History* 18 (February-March 1914).

Hannon, Patrick T. *The Biography of St. Bridget's Parish, West Rutland.* West Rutland Library, 1970 typescript.

———. *Historical Sketches on West Rutland: Celebrating Its Centennial, 1886–1986.* Edited by Victor Sevigny and Ethel Sevigny. Rutland, VT: Rutland Academy Books, 1986.

Harper's New Monthly Magazine 67, no. 302. "A Vacation in Vermont" (November 1883): 827.

Harveven, Tamara. *Family Time and Industrial Time: The Relationship Between the Family and Work in a New England Industrial Community.* New York: Cambridge University Press, 1982.

Hemenway, Abby Maria. *The History of Rutland County.* White River Junction, VT: White River Paper Company, 1882.

Herndon, Richard, comp. *Men of Progress: Biographical Sketches and Portraits of Leaders in Business and Professional Life in and of the State of Vermont.* Boston, MA: New England Magazine, 1898.

Higham, John. *Strangers in the Land: Patterns of American Nativism, 1860–1925.* New Brunswick, NJ: Rutgers University Press, 1988.

Hofstadter, Richard. *Great Issues in American History*, Vol. III. *From Reconstruction to the Present Day, 1864–1981*. N.p.: Vintage Publishers, 1982.

Humphrey, Zephine. *The Story of Dorset, Vermont*. Rutland, VT: Tuttle & Company, 1924.

Italian Aid Society. *Italian Aid Society, 1894–1994*. Rutland, VT: self-published, 1994.

Johnson, Curtis B., ed. *Historic Architecture of Rutland County*. Montpelier: State of Vermont, Division for Historic Preservation, 1988.

Johnson, Herbert W. "Our Swedish Pioneers." *Rutland Historical Society Quarterly* 13, no. 1 (Winter 1983): 26. Typescript of talk given at Proctor Historical Society on May 6, 1976.

———. *Proctor: My Home Town*. Rutland, VT: Academy Press, 1983.

Johnson, Otto. *Nineteen-Six in Vermont*. Proctor, VT: self-published, 1944.

Judd, Richard Munson. *The New Deal in Vermont: Its Impact and Aftermath*. New York: Garland Publishing, 1979.

Klyza, Christopher, and Stephen Trombulak. *The Story of Vermont: A Natural and Cultural History*. Hanover: University of New England Press, 1999.

Krause, Paul. *The Battle for Homestead, 1880–1892: Politics, Culture and Steel*. Pittsburgh, PA: University of Pittsburgh Press, 1992.

Kunin, Madeline M. *Living a Political Life*. New York: Knopf, 1994.

La Fayette, Wilbur. *Early History of Vermont*. Jericho, VT: Roscoe Printing House: 1899–1903.

Laurie, Bruce. *Artisans into Workers: Labor in Nineteenth-Century America*. New York: Noonday Press, 1989.

Leland, Ernest Stevens. "Barre: Cosmopolitan City and Granite Center of the World." *Vermont Life* 2, no. 1 (Fall 1947): 25.

MacKenzie, Katherine. *Indian Ways to Stage Coach Days: New Hampshire, Vermont, Quebec*. Ayers Cliff, Quebec: Pigwedgeon Press, 1996.

Mango, Helen, MD. "Interview on Geographic Formation of Vermont." Castleton State College Science Department, February 07, 2009.

Marburg, Anita. "Struggle in Marble." *Nation* 142 (April 1936).

McCusker, John J. "Comparing the Purchasing Power of Money in the United States (or the Colonies) from 1665 to Any Other Year, Including the Present." Economic History Services, http://www.measuringworth.com/ppowerus.

McKinney, J.P., comp. *The Industrial Advantages of the State of Vermont with the Material Development and Progress of the Principal Cities and Towns.* Rochester, NY: Commercial Publishing Company, 1890.

Montgomery, David. *Workers Control in America: Studies in the History of Work, Technology, and Labor Struggles.* New York: Cambridge University Press, 1979.

Montpelier Vermont Historical Society, comp. *Essays in the Early History of Vermont.* Montpelier: Montpelier Vermont Historical Society, 1943.

Office of the Vermont Secretary of State. Vermont State Archives, http://vermont-archives.org/govhistory/governance/Majority/pdf/1902.pdf.

"The Omaha Platform: Launching the Populist Party." History Matters. http://historymatters.gmu.edu/d/5361.

Omya in Vermont, http://www.omyainvermont.org.

Perkins, Nathan, Reverend. *A Narrative of Tour through the State of Vermont.* Woodstock, VT: self-published, 1920.

Petersen, James. *Otter Creek: The Indian Road.* Salisbury, VT: Dunmore History, 1990.

Ratti, Gino. "The Cesare Ratti Family of Proctor, Vermont." *Rutland Historical Society Quarterly* 20, no. 3 (1990).

Resch, Tyler. *The Bob Mitchell Years: An Anthology of a Half Century of Editorial Writing.* Rutland, VT: Rutland Herald, 1994.

———. *The Rutland Herald History.* Rutland, VT: Herald Association, 1995.

Rezneck, Samuel. "Unemployment, Unrest, and Relief in the United States During the Depression of 1893–1897." *Journal of Political Economy* 61 (1953).

Robinson, Rowland. *Vermont: A Study of Independence.* Boston, MA: Houghton Mifflin, 1892.

Rose, Virginia. *Emily Dutton Proctor: In Remembrance.* Privately published. Castleton State College Special Collections.

Rutland Historical Quarterly 12, no. 2. "Rutland's Mayors." (Spring 1982).

Sarca, Wayne A. "A Heritage Revealed: A Finn Grows Up in Rutland." *Rutland Historical Quarterly* 15, no. 1 (1985).

Sawyer, John E. "American Historians and the Business Elite" in *Men in Business: Essays on the Historical Role of the Entrepreneur.* Edited by William Miller. Cambridge, MA: Harvard University Press, 1952.

Schulberg, Budd. *Writers in America: Four Seasons of Success.* New York: Stein and Day, 1993.

Sherman, F. Barreda. *The Clements of Haverhill and Rutland, 1642–1969.* Mill Valley, CA: self-published, 1980.

Sherman, Jake. *Rutland Free Library 1886–1986, 100 Years of Service.* Typescript located in Rutland Library.

Sherman, Joe. *Fast Lane on a Dirt Road: Vermont Transformed, 1945–1990.* Woodstock, VT: Countryman Press, 1991.

Sherman, Michael, ed. *Vermont State Government Since 1965.* Burlington: University of Vermont, 1999.

Smith, Henry Perry, and William S. Rann, eds. *History of Rutland County, Vermont with Illustrations and Biographical Sketches of Some of the Prominent Men and Pioneers.* Syracuse, NY: Mason and Company, 1886.

Stillwell, Lewis D. *Migration from Vermont.* Montpelier: Vermont Historical Society and Rutland Vermont Academy Books, 1948.

Swan, Marvel G. *Early Families of Rutland, Vermont.* Rutland, VT: Rutland Historical Society, 1990.

Swift, Esther Munroe. *Vermont Place-Names: Footprints of History.* Brattleboro, VT: Stephen Greene Press, 1977.

Thompson, Zadock. *History of Vermont: Natural, Civil and Statistical in Three Parts, with a New Map of the State and 200 Engravings.* Burlington, VT: C. Goodrich, 1842.

Ullery, Jacob G., comp. *Men of Vermont: An Illustrated Biographical History of Vermonters and Sons of Vermont.* Compiled under the editorial supervision of Hiram A. Huse. Brattleboro, VT: Transcript Publishing Company, 1894.

Williamson, Samuel H. "What is Relative Value?" Economic History Services, http://measuringworth.com/calculators/uscompare.

Wilson, Harold Fisher. *The Hill Country of Northern New England: Its Social and Economic History, 1790–1930.* New York: Columbia University Press, 1936.

ABOUT THE AUTHOR

Mike Austin has been involved in higher education for over thirty years. He was nominated at Southern Illinois University for an Excellence in Teaching Award and received the Excellence in Teaching Award several times at the College of St. Joseph in Vermont. In addition, he has taught at Green Mountain College, Community College of Vermont and Castleton State College. His advanced degrees include a master's in English from Southern Illinois University and a PhD in history from the University of New Hampshire. His area of specialty is nineteenth-century American history, the Gilded Age.

Austin received the prestigious Charles Swain Thomas Award from the New England Association of Teachers of English. He is past president of the Vermont Council of Teachers of English, past president of the New England Association of Teachers of English and is current president of the Vermont Alliance for Social Studies. He has written extensively on the region and has directed many local, state and federal grants. He has been the past editor of the *Rutland Historical Quarterly*, and during his tenure as editor the *Quarterly* received several national awards for excellence in local history. He is a member of the Dimensions of Marble executive board.

In addition to his academic areas, Mike Austin has found time to act in many local theatre productions. His most recent performance was as the judge in *The Trial of Ebenezer Scrooge* for the acclaimed Actors Repertory Theatre of Vermont. An incurable romantic, he believes strongly in the sense of community and making the world a better place. And, just to warn you, he has an impish sense of humor and thinks that sharing and laughing is what life is all about.

Visit us at
www.historypress.net